DYNAMIC STUDIES
IN 1ST & 2ND
THESSALONIANS

BRINGING GOD'S WORD TO LIFE

FRED A. SCHEEREN

WESTBOW
PRESS®
A DIVISION OF THOMAS NELSON
& ZONDERVAN

WestBow Press books may be ordered through booksellers or by contacting:

WestBow Press
A Division of Thomas Nelson & Zondervan
1663 Liberty Drive
Bloomington, IN 47403
www.westbowpress.com
844-714-3454

Scripture marked (KJV) taken from the King James Version of the Bible.

Scripture quotations marked (NLT) are taken from the Holy Bible, New Living Translation, copyright ©1996, 2004, 2015 by Tyndale House Foundation. Used by permission of Tyndale House Publishers, Carol Stream, Illinois 60188. All rights reserved.

ISBN: 978-1-6642-5467-1 (sc)
ISBN: 978-1-6642-5466-4 (e)

Library of Congress Control Number: 2022901488

Print information available on the last page.

WestBow Press rev. date: 01/26/2022

DEDICATION

I DEDICATE THIS book to my lovely wife, Sally, who is a Jewish believer and Ivy League educated attorney. She has stood by me over the years and raised our sons in our God-loving home. The comfort of sharing our friendship and our love for Christ has encouraged me greatly in creating this series of dynamic studies of various books of the Bible. Sally's participation in our small group studies has added a much deeper dimension of richness to the discussions. Thank you for sharing your heritage, training, and knowledge.

CONTENTS

ACKNOWLEDGMENTS

MY FRIEND, BOB Mason, who at the time I began the Dynamic Bible Studies series was in his second career as the pastor of small groups at the Bible Chapel in the South Hills of Pittsburgh, suggested the overall structure of each study. Realizing our group was doing more in-depth work than most, he asked that I include several important segments in each lesson—most specifically, the warm-up and life application phases.

Bob suggested a great resource called the *New Testament Lesson Planner* from InterVarsity Press. I have augmented this with commentaries by Dr. Charles Missler from Koinonia House, the *Wiersbe Bible Commentary*, *The MacArthur Bible Handbook* by Dr. John MacArthur, the *Bible Commentaries* of J. Vernon McGee, and the whole of Scripture itself. To make the utilization of the whole of Scripture more efficient, I have also leaned heavily on the Libronix Digital Library, perhaps the most advanced Bible software available, and other resources to help us understand how the New Testament and the Tanakh (Old Testament) fit together as one cohesive document.

I have also enjoyed the input and encouragement of my friend, Ron Jones, as I have continued to prepare these studies. Ron is a former high school principal and administrator. He is also a committed believer and daily student of God's Word. His background in education coupled with his love of God and His Word has made him a powerful force for good.

I would like to express thanks to my late friend, Gordon Haresign, for his continued support and encouragement in my efforts to produce the Dynamic Bible Studies series. Gordon's journey began with his birth in the Belgian Congo. In the following years he was a senior executive with an international accounting firm, served in the military, labored as a Bible college professor, was instrumental in the leadership of a worldwide Bible correspondence school, and recently served as the Chairman of the Board of Directors of Scripture Union, an international Bible-based ministry. Gordon's work as a teacher, speaker, and missionary has taken him to over 50 countries on five continents. His three most recent books, *Authentic Christianity*, *Pray for the Fire to Fall* and his last work on Paul's letters to the Thessalonians which may someday be in print, should be required reading for all believers. Speaking of the Dynamic Bible Studies series he has written, "These are among the finest, if not the finest, inductive Bible studies available today. I strongly endorse them."

I would also like to express my appreciation to my two proof-readers. This includes:

- Cynthia Nicastro, an intelligent, ardent and devoted student of the Scriptures and a meticulous grammarian.

- My wife Sally, a Jewish believer and Ivy League educated lawyer who was law review in law school, worked for the Superior Court of the State of Pennsylvania, and is now in private practice.

May God bless you, inspire you, teach you, and change your life for the better as you work through these lessons.

Welcome to what I hope you find to be a most enjoyable and enlightening study of two letters written by one of the most intelligent, highly educated, well-read and influential men in history. This man's life was changed from that of a zealous, violent, murderous enemy of the early Jewish and Gentile believers to one of the most dedicated followers of the Jewish Messiah. These letters are part of the group of documents that today is known as "The Bible" and are referred to as the Books of First and Second Thessalonians.

As we consider how these books of the Bible fit into the whole of the New Testament and the Tanakh (the name used by Jews for the Old Testament, used here to emphasize the Jewishness of the Scriptures), we need to realize a number of things. We should stand in awe of this collection of 66 books, written over thousands of years by at least 40 different authors. Every detail of the text is there by design. It explains history before it happens, and comes to us from outside the dimension of time. It is, in short, the most amazing, most authenticated, and most accurate book available in the world.

If this claim is not strong enough, add to it the indisputable fact that the words contained therein have changed more lives than any others now in existence.

While the Judeo-Christian Scriptures are demonstrably perfect, my prepared studies are not. There is no way I or anyone else could possibly incorporate the depth of the text into individual sessions. I simply desire to provide a vehicle for others to use in their investigation of the Scriptures as they incorporate these timeless truths into their lives.

Speaking of small groups, Dr. Chuck Missler, a former Fortune 500 CEO, said, "I experienced more growth in my personal life as a believer by participating in small group Bible studies than anything else." I believe you may find this to be true in your experience and encourage you to be an active participant in such a mutually supportive, biblically-based group.

GROUND RULES

I DESIGNED THE first portion of each study to encourage readers to think about their personal situation. I designed the second portion to help people understand what the text says and how it relates to the whole of Scripture. And finally, each lesson ends with a discussion designed to help people apply that lesson.

You will notice that, in most instances, I have included the citation, but not the actual text of the Scripture we are considering. I did this on purpose. I believe we all learn more effectively if we have to dig out the text itself. As a byproduct of that exercise, we become more familiar with this marvelous book.

Scripture references are preceded or followed by a question or series of questions. Again, this is on purpose. I have also found that people seem to learn most effectively when employing the Socratic Method. That is, instead of telling someone what the text says and how it relates to other texts and life, they will remember it better if they answer questions about it and ferret out the information for themselves.

In a few instances, I have inserted additional commentary or partial answers to some of the questions to help the group get the most out of the study.

It is my intention and suggestion that the various scripture references be read out loud as part of each session. Shorter passages might be read by one participant, while anything over two or three verses might serve everyone better if one member reads one verse and another reads the next until the passage is completed. This keeps everyone involved. After reading these passages, I intend that how they relate to the primary Scripture at hand be seriously considered. At times, this relationship seems to be available and obvious on the surface. In many other instances, the interconnectedness of the whole of Scripture and its principles are most effectively understood through deeper thought, discussion, and prayer.

In commenting on and discussing the various passages, questions, concepts, and principles in this material, it is not required that any particular person give his or her input. The reader of any passage may, but is not pressured to, give his or her thoughts to the group. This is a group participation exercise for the mutual benefit of all involved and many people in the group giving their insight into a certain verse or question will often enhance the learning experience.

I also have two practical suggestions if you work through this book in a small group setting. Every time you meet, I suggest you review the calendar and agree upon the next scheduled meeting as well as who will bring refreshments. This will help the group to run a lot more smoothly while enhancing everyone's enjoyment, experience, and expectations.

Introduction to the Thessalonian Letters

So what's the big deal about Thessalonica?

"Modern" day readers around the world often wonder why Paul, perhaps the most intelligent, well-read and most highly educated man of his time, would bother to write not just one, but two letters to the people living in this ancient city.

To understand why he did so one must understand the city and its place at the time and in history.

Upon investigation we find Thessalonica was founded in 315 B.C. by Cassander. Cassander was the son-in-law of Philip of Macedonia. He was married to the half-sister, by the name of Thessalonike, of Alexander the Great. Cassander served as one of Alexander's four key generals and named his new city after his wife.

The city prospered. It sported a natural harbor at the head of the Thermaic Gulf. As such, it was situated directly on the main route between Rome and the East.

Cicero was reportedly in exile there in 58 B.C. (Marcus Tullius Cicero was a Roman statesman, lawyer and philosopher who played an important role in the politics in the later days of the Roman Republic. He tried, without success, to uphold republican principles during the turmoil that led to the establishment of the Roman Empire.)

During the struggles surrounding the establishment of the Roman Empire, the city leaders cooperated with Marc Antony and Caesar Augustus (known during the time of the struggles as Octavius). Because of the Thessalonian support of these notables of history against the almost equally known Cassius and Brutus, Rome declared Thessalonica to be a free city, like Athens.

As a free city, the Thessalonians were essentially permitted to rule themselves in terms of their internal affairs. Their overseers, called "politarchs," functioned as magistrates and were chosen from the ranks of what has been termed a "people's assembly." Consequently, no Roman soldiers were stationed there, although there was never any doubt that the city existed and operated at the pleasure of the Roman Empire.

As time passed it became the largest city in Macedonia by population and in Paul's day is assumed to have had a population of about 200,000. While the metropolis operated as a free city, the leaders were acutely aware of their somewhat tenuous position with Rome. They had to accord Rome homage or risk their perceived freedom.

While there were many heathen temples in this city, there was only one Synagogue of which we are aware. It was into this environment that Paul entered as an "itinerant preacher" but tentmaker by trade. We must be cautious about labeling Paul as an itinerant preacher as he was so much more in terms of education, intellectual competence, and ultimately world history.

It was Paul's knowledge of the existent Word of God, known as the Tanakh (which we call the Old Testament) that led to so much change, upheaval and conflict in the first century A.D. He served as a vital part of the vanguard who clearly explained that Jesus Christ was the Jewish Messiah promised for thousands of years.

When a person then trusted in Jesus as Lord they began to run into problems with the Roman overseers. The Romans taught that Caesar was the supreme lord and did not take it lightly when someone founded and acted otherwise. Indeed, as we see in a study of the book of Revelation, the time would come when those not willing to annually acknowledge this with a pinch of incense on an altar would be subject to execution. (Polycarp, an early leader of the church in Smyrna was burned at the stake for just such an "infraction.") The city leaders in Thessalonica feared losing their "free" status if they and their citizens did not proffer appropriate obsequiousness to the Roman Emperor.

As a result of the work of Paul and his compatriots, many Jews and then Gentiles trusted in the Jewish Messiah. As they studied the Scriptures they learned about more than the first coming of Jesus which was either mentioned or alluded to over 300 times. They also read about His second coming. As noted by the late Gordon Haresign, Chairman of the Board of Scripture Union, in his excellent book *Living in Anticipation of Our Lord's Return: An Exegetical and Devotional Commentary on Paul's Letters to the Thessalonians*, "scholars have identified over 1,800 references to Christ's second coming in the Bible." Indeed, it is mentioned in 17 of 39 books in the Old Testament and in 23 of the 27 books in the New Testament.

This was obviously an important part of the teaching and understanding of "early" believers. Such a position is evident from beginning to end in the New Testament documents and is particularly at the fore in the letters to the Thessalonians. It ties in with other biblical themes including the eventual appearing of an imposter sometimes known as the "lawless one" throughout prophetic references in the biblical record.

While many cities of antiquity have passed into obscurity, Thessalonica has not. It has survived great fires, invasions, battles as well as bombings in the Second World War. It is currently regarded as the second most important city in Greece with a population of over one million residents in the metropolitan area and is most often referred to as Thessaloniki or by its Anglicized name, Salonica (or Salonika). Its most prominent industries today are shipping, trade, banking and tobacco.

The first letter to the Thessalonians is actually the first of the New Testament documents to be written down. It was penned less than 20 years after the resurrection of Jesus Christ. Every chapter refers to His second coming.

Students of the Scriptures will also note that the topic of certainty resurfaces a number of times for the Thessalonians. Believing that all of God's Word is there by design I have followed Paul's example and purposely reviewed the assurance believers have several times over.

THANKFUL FOR YOU
1 THESSALONIANS 1:1-10

Open in Prayer

Group Warm-Up Questions

Who, in your opinion, are the best role models for other people?

What does it take for someone to make a lasting impression on you?

What causes a person to really change his or her attitudes and behavior?

Read: 1 Thessalonians 1:1-10

Reread: 1 Thessalonians 1:1

Who wrote this letter?

Note: While most people are generally acquainted with Paul, perhaps the most intelligent and well-educated man of his time, most are not as familiar with Silas. (Silas, along with Timothy, joined him in sending this letter.) Silas was:

1. An accomplished preacher and co-worker of Timothy and Paul.

    - See Acts 18:5 and 2 Corinthians 1:19.

2. A highly respected leader and member of the Jerusalem Council.

    - See Acts 15:22.

3. A prophet who spoke forth the Word of God and encouraged other believers.

    - See Acts 15:32.

4. In complete agreement with the decision of the Council regarding the new Gentile believers.

    - See Acts 15:22-32.

5. The person to whom Peter dictated his first letter and wrote it down for him. A person acting in this capacity is referred to as an *amanuensis*.

    - See 1 Peter 5:12.

Timothy was a Jew steeped in the Old Testament Scriptures, which the Jews call the Tanakh. His mother was Jewish and his father was Greek. (Acts 16:1) As a result of the influence of his godly believing mother and grandmother as well as Timothy's familiarity with the Old Testament prophecies about the Jewish Messiah, he became a believer. He became a protégé, friend, fellow warrior and frequent companion of Paul.

This was quite the all-star team.

To whom was this letter written?

What was wished for the recipients of the letter?

How might you describe the things wished for these people in your own words?

Reread: 1 Thessalonians 1:2

What did the writers of this letter do on behalf of the believers in Thessalonica?

How often were they doing this? What do you take the verbiage used in the text to mean?

For whom should we be doing this on a regular basis?

Should we also do this for ourselves?

Note: There is an almost magical, although I hesitate to use the adjective *magical*, result of doing this for other people on a consistent and ongoing basis. I first realized this when as a relatively new believer I agreed to take part in an all-night prayer vigil. I took this seriously. This took place in the lobby of a large Presbyterian church with perhaps 1,000 members. While I can't remember the national crisis that precipitated the call for this event, likely the difficulties associated with the Vietnam War, I do remember what the attendance at the vigil was like. As I recollect, there were at the most, eight of us.

While one could pray standing or sitting in a pew, we also had a portable contraption with a cushion to kneel on and a shelf to lean on. I really appreciated this contraption and I'm sure there is some proper name for it.

In any case, while I was a young believer, I was still facing some difficult things in my life. I had to continually re-appropriate the inner peace and wisdom offered and promised in John 16:33 and James 1:5. While God delivered these to me as promised through the power of the Holy Spirit (John 14:26 and 1 Corinthians 2:6-12), I discovered an amazing psychological, mental and spiritual result of praying for others.

As I went through the long night praying for other people, eating pizza, and praying again I noticed some very surprising things taking place. I prayed for just about every person and situation in the world that I could think of. I prayed primarily for their relationship with God, but also every other aspect of their lives. Gradually, as I did this, my seemingly large troubles seemed very small. While I did gladly receive further wisdom from this for my own situation in concert with the Scriptures, I also felt much less pressure about the situations I faced. I came away with a much greater sense of God's peace in my life and His power and at the same time a greater caring for others.

What do you make of this?

Have you ever had a similar experience?

What happened?

Note: Thankfulness on a continual basis is to be a priority for believers. See:

- 1 Thessalonians 5:18.

- 2 Corinthians 4:15.

- 2 Corinthians 9:11.

If you had to summarize, how might you describe the impact of being thankful and expressing it both on:

1. A person who does it?

2. Those who receive or observe it?

Reread: 1 Thessalonians 1:3

What specific three things about the Thessalonian believers made a lasting impression on Paul, Silas and Timothy?

1.

2.

3.

Note: Be sure to read this verse in several versions. The last item on the list is sometimes summarized in more paraphrased versions as "enduring hope." However, a literal reading of the original language reveals that this particular mention of hope refers not only to true biblical hope of a believer (as noted below), but a forward looking anticipation of the return of Jesus Christ. This is indeed a full and motivating "hope."

Biblical hope: The use of the word "hope" in the Greek is the opposite of our use of the word in English. In the Greek, "hope" is a confidence, sureness, and knowledge of future things. In fact, in the Greek, the word "hope" infers a certainty stronger than knowing. It is an ultimate, internal, overpowering, all-enveloping eternal surety and truth that is absolute.

It is interesting to see that faith, hope and love are interrelated and compliment each other. See:

- 1 Thessalonians 5:8.

- 1 Corinthians 13:13.

- Galatians 5:5.

- Colossians 1:4.

- Hebrews 6:10-12.

- Hebrews 10:22-24.

- 1 Peter 1:21.

Why do you think this interrelationship exists?

How do you see it working out in the lives of believers when experienced as God intends?

Reread: 1 Thessalonians 1:4

What two things did Paul, Silas and Timothy say they knew about the believers in Thessalonica?

1.

2.

Note: Election in the Old Testament was generally understood as a national matter. Indeed the promises of a specific area of land to Israel were made over 200 times. This does not, of course, negate God's utilization of certain men and women as His agents in the Tanakh.

In the New Testament we achieve a fuller understanding of this. (We must remember that the New and Old Testaments fit together like a hand in a glove.) It is said that the Old Testament is revealed in the new, while the new is concealed in the old. There is really no need for any division between the Old and the New. Together they form one cohesive document we know as the Bible.

We see what at first glance appears to be God's unilateral choosing of certain individuals in the following verses:

John 13:18

John 15:16

Acts 9:15

James 2:5

2 Peter 1:10

However, there is more at work in this construct.

Read: Ephesians 1:4

What did God do before the world was created?

What did God intend to be the result of His action?

In his book *Evangelism and the Sovereignty of God*, J. I. Packer states that the sovereignty of God and man's responsibility is an antinomy--an appearance of contradiction between conclusions which seem equally logical, reasonable or necessary (p. 18). He continues to say that while God "orders and controls all things, human actions among them . . . He holds every man responsible for the choices he makes and the courses of action he pursues" (p.22).

<u>Reread</u>: John 6:36-40

<u>Question</u>: What promise do we see for those who come to trust in Jesus?

<u>Question</u>: How did Jesus summarize His Father's will?

<u>Note:</u> This passage contains some concepts that are sometimes, on the surface, difficult for those of us with finite minds to understand. We see:

1. God's promise to those who come to Jesus.

2. The concept that one must come to Jesus to receive life.

3. The statements about those who have come to Him and are going to come to Him. (He already knows.)

4. The statement that the Lord wants all men and women to come to Him.

This seeming conundrum can be more fully understood as one studies the Scriptures and views them a whole. In other words:

1. God wants all people to come to Him.

2. We must choose to come to Him.

3. The "elect" will come to Him.

4. God knows who will come to Him.

We can see this borne out in the following verses:

John 17:2

John 17:6

John 17:9

John 17:11-12

John 17:24

Ephesians 1:4

2 Thessalonians 2:13

1 Timothy 2:3-4

Luke 19:10

2 Peter 3:9

We also see that God makes a bona fide offer to every person in the following verses:

John 3:16

John 3:36

John 5:24

Romans 10:9

Romans 10:13

We see the concept of this antinomy working in John 6:37 where we find that all that come are received and all that are given come.

Some people find it helpful to think of this in terms of a "life parade." Imagine God, who is not bound by the constraints of time, flying in a helicopter high above a parade of the events that make up your life. He knows the beginning from the end, He knows the way He wants you to go, and yet you have a choice.

Does this concept seem difficult to understand? No wonder.

See:

- Isaiah 55:8-9

- Ephesians 3:18

Read: Ephesians 1:5

What did God decide in advance for those who come to Him by trusting in Yeshua Hamaschiah, the Jewish Messiah, who we know as Jesus?

Let's take a moment and further attempt to make two words about the future, God's foreknowledge and their meaning more clear, drawing upon insights from Warren Wiersbe.

1. The first word is "predestination." As this word is used in the Bible it refers primarily to what God does and will do for people who have come to know Him through a personal relationship with Jesus Christ. <u>Nowhere in the Judeo Christian Scriptures does it indicate that anyone is predestined to hell. The word is used only in relationship to God's people.</u> For example, God's purpose for history and believers as He has already decided relates to:

- The crucifixion (Acts 4:25-28).

- Our adoption into the family of God (Ephesians 1:5).

- Our conformity to Jesus (Romans 8:29-30).

- Our future inheritance (Ephesians 1:11).

2. The second word is election, which refers to people, their choices and God's foreknowledge as already discussed.

We should then realize that:

1. Nobody is saved without choosing to be saved. Nobody is lost without choosing to be lost.

2. God's desire is to save as many people as possible, not as few people as possible. We see this truth all over the pages of God's Word.

Reread: 1 Thessalonians 1:5

What four things characterized the way in which Paul, Silas and Timothy brought the Good News to the Thessalonians?

1.

2.

3.

4.

How did the Thessalonians know that what they heard from their three visitors was true?

What difference do we see between times when God's Word is presented with conviction and power and times when it is not?

Note: God's Word and His Holy Spirit must be intertwined as God intended.

Please read the following verses and summarize your understanding of this:

Ephesians 6:17

1 Thessalonians 4:8

2 Thessalonians 2:13

1 Thessalonians 5:19

It has been said that:

The Spirit without the Word is weaponless;

The Word without the Spirit is powerless.

It has also been said that:

Bible reading without prayer can be atheistic;

Prayer without the Bible is presumptuous.

What do you think of these statements?

Are they true or partially true? How so?

Reread: 1 Thessalonians 1:6

What happened in the lives of the Thessalonians when they received the message brought to them?

1.

2.

3.

Do people who make a decision to follow Jesus today sometimes face suffering or difficulty in their lives like that experienced by the Thessalonians? How so?

Note: Chuck Missler thought that the Gospel aroused hostility because it challenges human pride and self-indulgence.

What do you think about what Chuck said?

Do you think a decision to trust Jesus Christ is worth any suffering experienced? Why or why not?

Reread: 1 Thessalonians 1:7

What was the result of what happened in the lives of the Thessalonian believers?

Is it normally evidence of a healthy life as a believer when it becomes an example to others? How so?

Reread: 1 Thessalonians 1:8

What else happened beyond the initial impact on believers throughout Madedonia and Achaia? (Macedonia and Achaia were the northern and southern provinces into which the Romans divided the territory of the Greeks.)

1.

2.

3.

Note: The Greek word translated as ringing out in some versions is *execheo*. This is derived from the word *echos* and means a loud noise, trumpet, or thunderclap.

Understanding this definition, what further insight do you have into the impact the believers in Thessaloniaca were having upon all of Greece?

Reread: 1 Thessalonians 1:9-10

What four things were people talking about as they referred to the believers in Thessalonica?

1.

2.

3.

4.

When others see these things in the lives of believers, what part does it play in showing them the truth of God's Word?

Reread: 1 Thessalonians 1:10

To what very specific things were the Thessalonians looking forward?

Reread: 1 Thessalonians 1:4

After going through the primary passage under consideration today it is obvious that as Paul stated in the verse we just read that certain things made it glaringly obvious that God had chosen the Thessalonians for His purposes.

Please reread 1 Thessalonians 1:4-10 and list the things you see that helped Paul and/or any other observer come to this conclusion.

1.

2.

3.

4.

5.

6.

7.

8.

9.

10.

11.

12.

How did this work? What made non-believers understand that something special had happened in the lives of the believers?

What about you?

Do you feel that God has chosen you for His purposes?

How do you see this evidenced in your life in a fashion that is consistent with what we see in Scripture?

What characteristics in a person's life would convince you that a person genuinely has become a believer and is following God?

Does the faith that one has depend upon the actions of those who claim to be believers or is there something more? Please read the following verses as you construct your answer.

John 14:6

2 Timothy 3:16-17

2 Timothy 1:7

Galatians 5:22-23

Application Questions

How can you be more of a model to other believers this week?

In what way can you present the truth of God's Word and the life He offers to others with power and conviction the next time you share it?

Close in Prayer

PURE MOTIVES IN ACTION
1 THESSALONIANS 2:1-16

Open in Prayer

Group Warm-Up Questions

How do you know when someone is trying to use flattery to manipulate you?

What are signs of genuine love between a parent and a child?

What qualities should a leader among believers have?

Read: 1 Thessalonians 2:1-16

Reread: 1 Thessalonians 2:1

What did the Thessalonians know about the visit from Paul, Silas, and Timothy?

Reread: 1 Thessalonians 2:13

How was the impact of the work of these men successfully measured?

How can the impact of our work as representatives of the God of the Universe be assessed?

When is this evident?

Do we always get to see the results in the near term?

Will there be results?

Read Isaiah 55:11 as you construct your answer.

Reread: 1 Thessalonians 2:2

Under what conditions did this all-star team of believers share the truth of God's Word with the Thessalonians?

What kind of opposition can we expect when we:

1. Speak out for Jesus Christ?

2. Simply live by God's standards as clearly stated in His Word in opposition to the standard of the culture?

3. Stand up and speak out for Biblical principles in our daily lives?

Reread: 1 Thessalonians 2:3

Note: The Greek used in this verse would also be used for "catching fish with bait."

Reread: 1 Thessalonians 2:3-5

What false charges were made against Paul, Silas and Timothy?

How was it that these three believers were able to share God's Good News despite great opposition?

Read the following verses as you put together your answer.

Read:

Isaiah 41:13

Psalm 27:1

1 Peter 5:7

Psalm 56:3

Matthew 6:25-27

Matthew 6:34

Psalm 121:1-2

James 1:2-4

Romans 8:17-18

James 1:12

Proverbs 3:5-6

Psalm 46:1

Romans 8:28

2 Timothy 1:7

Philippians 4:11-13

Philippians 1:27-28

2 Thessalonians 3:3

Joshua 1:9

Deuteronomy 31:6, 8

1 Corinthians 15:57

1 John 4:4

Reread: 1 Thessalonians 2:4

Also read: Galatians 1:10

Who were Paul, Silas and Timothy trying to please?

Who is it that examines the motives of our hearts?

How does this make you feel to know that the God of the Universe, who knows all and cannot be deceived, will be doing this?

How do the opinions of others impact how we share our faith?

Read the following verses as you construct your answer.

Colossians 4:5-6

1 Corinthians 9:20-22

1 Corinthians 10:33

Romans 15:2

How can we be sure to remain faithful and obedient while engaging in these interactions?

See 1 Thessalonians 5:16-22 and 2 Timothy 3:16-17 as you put together your answer.

Reread: 1 Thessalonians 2:4

It has been said that the most dangerous type of preaching is that which is partly true.

What are your thoughts about this?

If you believe the statement to be correct, why do you feel that way?

Reread: 1 Thessalonians 2:4

Also read:

Psalm 17:3

Jeremiah 11:20

Acts 1:24

Who is it who examines our hearts and motives?

How does it make you feel that this is true and that we can't fool God?

In the face of these truths, why do some people still try and fool God?

Reread: 1 Thessalonians 2:5

How were other traveling religious teachers deceiving people?

Does this kind of thing happen today? Can you think of examples?

Reread: 1 Thessalonians 2:5

What kind of praise were Paul, Silas and Timothy not seeking for themselves.

Also read: Colossians 3:23-24

What kind of recognition were these three men seeking?

Should we do the same?

How does this work itself out in daily life?

Reread: 1 Thessalonians 2:6

From who were the members of Paul's team seeking affirmation?

How can a desire for popularity (even among believers) twist one's desire and commitment to serve God?

How can we be sure that we are following the admonition in 1 Thessalonians 2:4?

Reread: 1 Thessalonians 2:7

How did Paul describe the relationship he and his team had with the Thessalonians?

Reread: 1 Thessalonians 2:8

What were Paul and his companions delighted to do?

Reread: 1 Thessalonians 2:9

What did Paul want the Thessalonians to remember about his time with them?

Also Read:

2 Corinthians 11:9

2 Thessalonians 3:8

Acts 18:3

Acts 20:34

1 Corinthians 9:11-12

Why was it important that Paul and his compatriots provided their own living without relying on the Thessalonians?

When do we see this kind of thing in the world today?

Why does it have an especially powerful impact?

Do you think it makes a greater impression on a nonbeliever when successful believers share their faith with them than when a minister paid to do so does it?

Why is this?

Read: Colossians 4:5-6

Mark 16:15-16

Matthew 28:19-20

What does this make you think about the importance of sharing one's faith with those around them?

Have you seen believing participants in unpaid biblically oriented positions sharing their faith?

Please discuss some examples and the impact you have seen this have.

Paul's financial independence and the message that it sent were important factors in his work. It:

1. Cut off criticism.

    • See 2 Corinthians 11:7-12.

2. Set a worthy example.

    • See 2 Thessalonians 3:7-9.

3. Showed his care and concern for them.

    • See 2 Corinthians 12:13-18.

4. Even allowed him to share with those less fortunate than he.

    • See Acts 20:34-35

Reread: 1 Thessalonians 2:10

How did Paul describe the way that he and his companions acted toward the believers in Thessalonica?

The Scripture lists three characteristics of the way he, Silas and Timothy acted toward the believers on their visit. What were they?

1.

2.

3.

Why was this so impactful and important?

What standards of behavior and care should believers today follow as they try to reach out to people?

Reread: 1 Thessalonians 2:11-12

In what ways did Paul and his team treat each one of the Thessalonians as a father ideally treats his children? Please make a list.

1.

2.

3.

Why is it important that they treated each person individually in this fashion and not just the believers there as a group?

What can we learn from this in our lives?

Why is it important that we deal with people as unique individuals and not just part of some group?

What happens when a group of people is simply dealt with corporately and not as unique and valuable individuals?

How do you explain the fact that these characteristics of human behavior and guidelines are found not just in books on psychology and success, but have their root in timeless principles as set forth in the Word of God?

Reread: 1 Thessalonians 2:13

Also read: Acts 17:2-3

Note: At the time this letter was penned the Word of God in written form referred to the Old Testament, what Jews call the Tanakh. It now extends to 66 books written by 40 authors over thousands of years. Every word, every place name, every form of punctuation is there by design. It is an integrated message system from God Himself.

How did the Thessalonians receive the Word of God?

What is the difference between accepting a teaching as the Word of God and responding to it?

Read: Acts 17:11

How does the concept in this verse play into the way one receives or does not receive a teaching claiming to be from the Word of God?

Reread: 1 Thessalonians 2:14

In what way were the believers in Thessalonica like the groups of people following the Word of God and Jesus Christ in Judea?

Reread: 1 Thessalonians 2:15-16

What kind of opposition had Paul, Silas and Timothy faced?

What kind of opposition to believers today sometimes face?

Has this ever happened to you? Please explain.

Note: Quite obviously, Paul was a Jew among the Jews and his companions joining him in writing this letter were the same. However, he is quite upset with any Jews trying to stop Gentiles from hearing the Good News. This was counter to the early believers as a whole as we see at the Jerusalem Council (see Acts 11:1-18).

Some of the Jews, as Paul writes, even killed some of the prophets and were instrumental in the death of Jesus, King of the Jews and the Jewish Messiah. However, this does not negate the fact that Israel and the Jews are the apple of God's eye (see Zechariah 2:8), His Chosen People, used for the transmission and spreading of his word, and playing an important role throughout all of history, including the future. (See 144,000 Jews playing a vital role in history to come in Revelation 7:4-8 and the New Jerusalem Revelation in 21:1-5.)

Further note: On May 14, 1948 Israel was reestablished as a nation exactly as foretold in the Old Testament. They have made the land bloom as predicted, put their enemies to flight, and become a blessing to the world through their many scientific discoveries and advances.

Reread: 1 Thessalonians 2:16

What is God's response to people who oppose the sharing, preaching and spreading of His Word and His Gospel?

Application Questions

In what ways can you share your life with others in your efforts to share the Good News of the Gospel and a personal relationship with Jesus Christ?

What can you do this week to be sure you are trying to please God and not people?

Close in Prayer

WEEK 3

CONCERN FOR THE THESSALONIANS
1 THESSALONIANS 2:17-3:5

Open in Prayer

Group Warm-Up Questions

If you were accused of a crime you didn't commit, how would you respond?

How do you encourage a friend who is feeling down and hopeless?

Read: 1 Thessalonians 2:17-3:5

Reread: 1 Thessalonians 2:17

How did Paul describe his team's departure and separation from the Thessalonians?

Note: Paul and his team had only been with the Thessalonians for about three weeks. Now, after an absence of about 9 months, they still retain great ties and concern for these people.

How do you explain this?

Reread: 1 Thessalonians 2:18

What stopped Paul from returning to Thessalonica when he tried?

How does Satan attempt to stop or hinder our efforts or plans for God?

Does he ever use misdirection? How so?

Does he ever use pride? How so?

Does he ever use a person's neglect to read their Bible on a daily basis? How so?

Does he use a person's neglect of their prayer life? How so?

Does he use a person's neglect to fellowship with other believers? How so?

What other tools does Satan sometimes use?

Reread: 1 Thessalonians 2:19

What personal impact did the Thessalonians have on Paul and his team?

What did Paul say would be his team's crown and reward at the return of Jesus Christ?

How can investing your life in someone pay eternal dividends?

Have you ever seen this in your life and relationships? What happened?

Which of our personal accomplishments will count for something when we stand in the presence of Christ?

We should note that there are five crowns mentioned in Scripture. Please look these up and discuss what they mean to you. They are:

1. The crown of righteousness.

    •   See 2 Timothy 4:8.

2. The crown of glory and honor.

    •   See 1 Peter 5:2-4.

3. The crown of life.

    •   See Revelation 2:10.

4. The incorruptible crown.

    •   See 1 Corinthians 9:25-27.

5. The crown of rejoicing.

    •   See 1 Thessalonians 2:19-20.

Reread: 2 Timothy 4:8

When are these crowns received?

Why do we often hear a misnomer at funerals when someone says that the departed has gone to their reward?

Reread: 1 Thessalonians 2:20

How did Paul describe the Thessalonians in this verse?

Why did he feel this way?

Reread: 1 Thessalonians 3:1-2

What did Paul and his team decide to do?

How did Paul describe Timothy?

What was the stated purpose of Timothy's visit?

What practical things can we do to encourage and strengthen others in their faith?

Note: Strengthening other believers was important to Paul and his compatriots. Read the following verses to see this:

Acts 15:32

Acts 15:41

Acts 16:5

Acts 18:23

Romans 1:11

Romans 16:25

Is such strengthening equally important today? Why?

Read 2 Timothy 1:7

Who, in the end, is the source of this strength?

Reread: 2 Thessalonians 3:3

For what other reason was Timothy sent to visit the Thessalonians?

What did Paul say about trials?

Note: Trials and tribulations, while not normally welcomed by us, are used by God in the life of a believer. What the enemy intends for evil is used by God for good. We can see this principle in Genesis 50:20 and repeated time and again in Scripture. Please read the following verses and discuss what we learn from them:

Matthew 5:10-12

John 16:33

2 Timothy 2:10-13

1 Peter 4:12-14

Isaiah 41:10

James 1:3-4

Romans 5:3-5

Dr. Chuck Missler, one of the greatest Biblical scholars to ever live, said that there were very few mistakes he missed in his life, yet it was by all counts exemplary. Other believers have said that they learned a lot in life, often by doing it wrong in the first place.

What are your thoughts about this?

Is this God using what our enemy intended for evil for good?

Reread: 2 Thessalonians 3:4

What warning did Paul, Silas and Timothy give the Thessalonian believers on their previous visit?

Why was Paul concerned that trials and troubles might undercut the faith of the Thessalonians?

Does this ever happen to people? How so?

Reread: 2 Thessalonians 3:5

What did Paul want Timothy to find out on his trip?

What was Paul concerned about?

How could you help a young believer whose faith has been damaged by opposition or discouragement?

Application Questions

What younger believer can you help get established in the faith? How?

This week, how can you resist the temptations that hinder your spiritual progress?

Close in Prayer

AN ENCOURAGING REPORT
1 THESSALONIANS 3:6-13

Open in Prayer

Group Warm-Up Questions

If you could make a surprise visit to a dear friend or relative, whom would you select?

How can you express love to someone when you can't see or talk to the person?

Read: 1 Thessalonians 3:6-13

Reread: 1 Thessalonians 3:6

What were the first four bits of good news that Timothy brought back?

1.

2.

3.

4.

Reread: 1 Thessalonians 3:7

What other key factor did Timothy report about the Thessalonians?

How did this part of the news particularly impact Paul and those with him?

Why do you think this particular characteristic of the Thessalonian believers is both singled out and brought such encouragement to the other believers to whom it was reported?

Reread: 1 Thessalonians 3:8

What particular aspect of the Thessalonian's faith and lives was so positively cited in this verse?

How did Paul further describe the impact of this report and characteristic?

What do you think he meant by what he said?

Read: Philippians 1:21

How do you relate this to 1 Thessalonians 3:8?

How would you define and evaluate the depth of a person's faith?

This is an important question as we examine our own lives and those around us. The incorrect notion or lie that those following Jesus Christ should not discern right from wrong has been responsible for the decline of the culture where it has been applied.

Unbelievers, if they know one verse, often love to quote Matthew 7:1 and take it to mean that there are no standards of behavior to which one can hold oneself or others. (For greater context see the full quote in Matthew 7:1-3.)

This is, of course, patently misunderstood and quoted out of context. As we have said before, one verse theology is essentially no theology at all. God's Word must be viewed and understood as a whole and must not be twisted by human emotions and desires.

In the Nazarene denomination this was often summarized by telling parishioners that while they were not to judge people, they were to be fruit inspectors.

So what is a believer to do?

First, we must realize that Biblical standards of conduct, speech, behavior, relationships and life are rampant in the New and Old Testaments. When these principles are applied to one's life the result is always good. Justice, truth, love, peace, joy, and fulfillment always follow although believers must take a stand for God's standards to make it happen.

Conversely, when these principles are violated, one reaps only negative consequences in the long run, despite possible periodic short term gains.

It is easy enough for a Biblically literate person to view their own life and know if they are exhibiting the fruit of the spirit as succinctly delineated in Galatians 5:22-23. If one does this they can then easily reapply the admonition found in this very letter in 1 Thessalonians 5:16-22.

Going a little bit further, read the following verses dealing with discernment and discuss what they mean to us as students of God's Word and followers of His plan and Messiah:

Romans 12:2

2 Timothy 3:16-17

Hebrews 4:12

1 Corinthians 2:14

Proverbs 8:8-9

Hosea 14:9

Romans 12:9

1 Kings 3:9-12

Proverbs 1:1-2

Proverbs 3:21-24

Ecclesiastes 12:13

Ephesians 4:14

Philippians 1:9-10

James 3:17

Reread: 1 Thessalonians 3:9

What was one of the aspects of the prayers of Paul and his companions?

How did this practice impact the people doing the praying?

How and why do you see this working out in real time?

Why does it bless someone when they spend time praying for the benefit of others?

Read: 1 Thessalonians 3:10-11

How often did Paul and those with him pray?

How did Paul characterize these ongoing prayers?

What request did Paul and his team make when praying?

Why were they so anxious to visit the Thessalonians again to help them with their faith and knowledge?

Read: 2 Corinthians 1:24

How does this relate to the concepts in 1 Thessalonians 3:10?

How do you show your concern for believers in distant places?

Read: 1 Thessalonians 5:17

How often should we be praying?

Read: Ephesians 3:20

What else happens when we pray?

Reread: 1 Thessalonians 3:12

For whom did Paul wish to see the love of the Thessalonians grow?

What two characteristics of this love did Paul mention?

1.

2.

What did he say about the love he and those with him had for the Thessalonians?

How would you define and evaluate the depth of a person's love?

How does a person's love increase?

Reread: 1 Thessalonians 3:13

What three results did Paul expect the Thessalonians to experience as their love grew?

1.

2.

3.

When, in particular, did Paul wish to see these things come to fruition?

What about the near term? Do you think he wished for them to experience these things in their daily lives in addition to the future? Why?

How can a person have their heart strengthened?

What, in this verse, does Paul say about the second coming of Jesus Christ?

If you had to make a list of the characteristics you expect of someone who is standing firm in the Lord, what would you include?

1.

2.

3.

4.

5.

6.

7.

8.

9.

10.

Many years ago young believers were sometimes asked "If you were arrested for being a believer, would there be enough evidence to convict you?"

What are your thoughts about this question?

Would there be enough evidence to convict you as a follower of Jesus Christ if you were arrested for it?

The definitive guide and answer to this and all other questions is the Word of God itself. Regardless of what any religious organization says, the Bible says in summary that a "real Christian" or follower of Jesus Christ:

1. Has personally accepted Jesus Christ as their savior.

2. Trusts in the death and resurrection of Jesus Christ alone for the forgiveness of their sins.

3. Has the Holy Spirit living within them.

4. Lives a life that evidences change consistent with trust in Jesus and the Word of God.

While this is a good summary, please confirm this with God's Word itself as we see in Acts 17:11. It is God's Word and not my summary upon which one should rely.

As a starter take a look at the following references:

1 John 2:6

Ephesians 2:8-9

Romans 10:9-11

1 Corinthians 15:3

1 Corinthians 15:13-14

Romans 8:9

Romans 8:15

2 Corinthians 5:17

James 2:18

John 8:12

Application Questions

What changes do you need to make to focus a significant part of your prayers on others?

What preparations can you make this week to get ready for Christ's return?

Close in Prayer

LIVING TO PLEASE GOD
1 THESSALONIANS 4:1-12

Open in Prayer

Group Warm-Up Questions

How much do you think people are influenced by what they see on television?

How is sex viewed by many of the people you know and work with?

Read: 1 Thessalonians 4:1-12

Reread: 1 Thessalonians 4:1

Also read: Romans 12:1-2

What instructions had Paul and his team given the Thessalonians when they were with them?

What do you think about the way Paul skillfully avoids criticizing the Thessalonians while encouraging them to do even better?

Why do you think he approaches the subject in this fashion and what is the impact?

How often do we need to be reminded about God's instructions for our lives?

How can believers effectively do this?

Read the following verses as you construct your answer:

Philippians 1:6

1 Peter 2:2-3

1 Timothy 4:6

Matthew 4:4

Hebrews 5:12-14

John 6:27

John 6:51

John 6:63

1 Corinthians 10:3-4

2 Timothy 3:16-17

Psalm 119:30

Psalm 119:9-10

Proverbs 30:5

Psalm 119:10-11

Psalm 1:2

Colossians 3:16

God's Word has been and is held in high regard by many great people. It is interesting to note that:

Charles Spurgeon is said to have pronounced that "Nobody ever outgrows Scripture; the book widens and deepens with our years."

Theodore Roosevelt reportedly said that "A thorough knowledge of the Bible is worth more than a college education."

Billy Graham is credited with saying "the very practice of reading [the Bible] will have a purifying effect upon your mind and heart. Let nothing take the place of this daily exercise."

What are your thoughts about what these well-known historical personages have said about this topic?

Reread: 1 Thessalonian 4:2

By whose authority did Paul's visiting trio give their instructions?

Reread: 1 Thessalonians 4:3

What is God's overriding desire for all believers? What does He want us to be?

What simple formula does he put forth to help achieve this standard?

How does this relate to our bodies?

Reread: 1 Thessalonians 4:4

If we follow God's simple plan for purity what are the three immediately observable results?

1.

2.

3.

Reread: 1 Thessalonians 4:5

How is the way those who do not know God treat the gift of sexuality characterized?

Read: 1 Corinthians 6:13-20

How does God want us to use our bodies?

Reread: 1 Thessalonians 4:6

What are believers commanded to never do?

Why was it necessary for this warning to be given?

This verse says that sexual sins are not victimless. Besides harming the instigator they harm the other person involved. Why do you think this biblical and psychological analysis of human behavior is so?

What is the consequence of violating these precepts? (It is worse than today's popular western culture might think.)

Read Romans 1:21-32 and Proverbs 5:1-14 as you construct your answer.

Have you ever observed what has happened in the lives of believers, or supposed believers when they violated God's principles for healthy marital relationships? What happened?

How would you respond to someone who says it is possible to be an obedient believer while also being sexually immoral?

Reread: 1 Thessalonians 4:7

What kind of lives had God called us to live?

What kind of lives has God most decidedly not called those who follow Him to live?

Reread: 1 Thessalonians 4:8

Whose teaching is being rejected by anyone refusing to obey the rules for successful relationships so clearly laid out in God's Word?

What does this have to do with the Holy Spirit?

How does the popular media in our culture attempt to influence people about sex and intimacy?

Read: 1 Thessalonians 5:19

Ephesians 4:29

How does suppressing the Holy Spirit impact the success a believer has in life?

Reread: 1 Thessalonians 4:9-10

Leviticus 19:18

Matthew 25:35

John 5:11-14

John 13:34-35

John 15:17

Galatians 5:14

1 Peter 4:8

1 John 3:14

1 John 3:23

What command of God were the Thessalonians known for obeying?

It is of great interest to note that Tertullian reportedly said "Behold how these Christians love one another."

Note: Quintus Septimius Florens Tertullianus, better known as Turtullian to us, is believed to have trained as a Roman lawyer. He lived at the end of the second century and the beginning of the third century AD. After committing his life to Jesus Christ he became a staunch and intellectually dominating defender of God's Word and faith in Him.

What can we do to foster such an observation by those who are not yet believers into reality today?

How is such an observation by an unbeliever much more effective and glorifying to God than an emphasis on ecclesiastical differences?

Why might opponents to faith in Jesus Christ try to find ways to highlight dissention among believers instead of love?

Reread: 1 Thessalonians 4:11

What ambition was the Thessalonians encouraged to pursue?

Are all believers to pursue this same ambition in whole or in part? How so?

It is also of interest to note that the Greeks looked down upon all physical labor. They felt it was to be done by slaves. The Word of God honors all forms of honest labor. We can see this in:

Colossians 3:17

Colossians 3:23-24

Ephesians 4:28

Mark 6:3

Reread: 1 Thessalonians 4:12

Why do you think Paul found it necessary to expound on the points he covers in today's primary passage in this letter?

What is the result when believers live their lives as God intends?

How are unbelievers impacted by this?

How can ambition for fame, success or wealth hurt a believer? Can you think of an example?

How can a biblical view of these things help a believer or enhance their witness? Please think of some examples.

Read: Colossians 4:5-6

How else are unbelievers affected when those following God live their lives as He intends?

When you envision a holy life, how do you imagine it?

What might motivate us to live lives that are holy?

Read the following verses for more perspective on this:

Leviticus 17:11

Isaiah 53

Jeremiah 11:19

John 1:29

John 3:16

John 10:10

2 Peter 3:10-13

Hebrews 10:1-18

Application Questions

In the future, how could you help a Christian caught in sexual sin?

What can you do to maintain your purity?

When can you spend some time examining your ambitions in light of God's priorities for you?

Close in Prayer

WEEK 6
THE COMING OF THE LORD
1 THESSALONIANS 4:13-5:11

Open in Prayer

Group Warm-Up Questions

How can the death of a loved one change a person's life?

How do you react when you hear predictions about the end of the world?

Driving Home the Concept of Biblical Hope:

In today's study we will visit, review, and then revisit the biblical concept of hope. Psychologists tell us that to remember something we do best if it is repeated three times. We also see this operant in God's Word. This is often borne out in speech preparation training where one is told to:

1. Tell your audience what you are going to tell them.

2. Tell them what you want them to know.

3. Tell your audience what you told them.

<u>Important Note</u>: The use of the word "hope" in the Greek is the opposite of our use of the word in English. In the Greek, "hope" is a confidence, sureness, and knowledge of future things. In fact, in the Greek, the word "hope" infers a certainty stronger than knowing. It is an ultimate, internal, overpowering, all-enveloping eternal surety and truth that is absolute.

Read: 1 Thessalonians 4:13-5:11

Reread: 1 Thessalonians 4:13

What concern was Paul addressing?

Who has no hope when they die?

Going back to the original language can be quite helpful and interesting as we see the emphasis God places on principles in His Word.

Let's take a look at 1 Thessalonians 4:13 in the KJV for an example of this. In that version the people who have no hope are referred to as "ignorant." The Greek word used is *Agnos* and the Latin translation is *Ignoramus*.

Please now read the following references in the KJV where the Greek word *Agnos* is used for a greater understanding of just what is being communicated to us:

1 Thessalonians 4:13

Romans 1:13

Romans 11:25

1 Corinthians 10:1

1 Corinthians 12:1

2 Corinthians 1:8

What lessons might one draw from this realization?

How certain is our hope?

Remember: We have the absolute certainty of Christ's death and resurrection. These events are incontrovertible historical facts. Observing the efforts of the Roman and Pharisaic authorities in the first century AD to suppress this truth, it was just pathetic and almost laughable to see them trying to hide the facts. There were just too many people around who had either seen these events themselves or knew someone who had.

Reread: 1 Thessalonians 4:13-14

How is the grief of a believer for a loved one who was also a believer different from an unbeliever?

How should a believer mourn the death of a fellow believer?

What happens when a believer dies?

Read the following two verses to aid in our understanding.

Philippians 1:23

2 Corinthians 5:8

Reread: 1 Thessalonians 4:15

What was the source of Paul's information about what happens to a believer who dies?

This is quite an interesting thing to observe. Here we have Paul, quite possibly the most intelligent and highly educated man of his day, who was intimately familiar with the scriptures, making this statement. He was inspired by God and used in penning the "God Breathed" words of much of the New Testament. Everything God used him to write was in direct confirmation of and coordination with the whole of Scripture which we know as the Bible. It is a matter of interest to also see:

Acts 9:5-6

Acts 22:17-21

Galatians 1:12

Galatians 2:2

And just so we are clear on this point, there is no new and contradictory or even confirming Scriptural revelation from God today as we see in Revelation 22:18-19.

We should note that in 1 Thessalonians 4:15 Paul is addressing the question of what happens to other believers who die before us. For further helpful insight into this please read:

2 Corinthians 5:4

1 Corinthians 15:49-52

This leads us into an examination that many people have had about what is sometimes referred to as one's "resurrection body."

We know:

1. Believers will be given new bodies like that of the Lord. See:

    *   Philippians 3:21

    *   1 John 3:2

2. One must die or be a participant in the *harpazo* or "rapture" to receive this body. Death is generally implied for most believers. See:

    *   Job 14:14

    *   Job 19:25-27

3. The Resurrection Body of Jesus Christ has a number of observable characteristics. See the following references and note what we learn:

- Luke 24:31

- John 20:19

- John 20:26

- Matthew 28:9

- Luke 24:36-42

- Luke 24:30-31

- Revelation 21:4

All things considered, how do you feel knowing that if you are a believer, your resurrection body will be even better than the best you have ever been in your time earth?

Reread: 1 Thessalonians 4:16-17

What sequence of immediate events will signal the Lord's return?

What hope do believers have in death?

Important Note: The use of the word "hope" in the Greek is the opposite of our use of the word in English. In the Greek, "hope" is a confidence, sureness, and knowledge of future things. In fact, in the Greek, the word "hope" infers a certainty stronger than knowing. It is an ultimate, internal, overpowering, all-enveloping eternal surety and truth that is absolute.

Read Titus 2:12-13 for further confirmation of the "hope" or absolute certainty and assurance that believers have.

How can the Words of today's scripture help a person who is grieving over someone who has died?

Why is the date and time of Christ's second coming of such interest to so many people?

We find the period of time immediately preceding His return for His followers in Matthew 24.

We also find amazingly rich information on prophecy and the future in God's Word itself.

In the book of Revelation, which is comprised of 404 verses, we find over 800 allusions to Old Testament Scripture.

Looking at the whole of Scripture we find that there are approximately 8,362 predictive verses in which 1,817 predictions are made about 737 separate matters.

When we look at the subject of Jesus Christ alone we find over 300 referenced to his first coming in the Old Testament. Amazingly, these have all been fulfilled in Him. This is obviously a statistical impossibility and in itself proves the mathematical certainty of the truth of Scripture and the identity of Jesus as the promised Jewish Messiah in whom any person can trust for their lives now as well as for eternal life. (See composite probability in the appendix to this book.)

Taking this one step even further, there are over 1,845 references to the second coming of Jesus Christ and His future rule on earth in the New and Old Testaments combined. This is mentioned in 17 books of the Old Testament and 23 of the 27 books in the New Testament.

From a statistical and mathematical view alone the biblical hope we have in Jesus Christ and the Word of God is incontrovertible.

Reread: 1 Thessalonians 4:18

What impact does God intend that knowing this part of His plan for believers should have upon them?

Can you think of an instance where this impact was borne out in real time? Please give an example.

Reread: 1 Thessalonians 5:1-2

How will the Lord return?

Reread: 1 Thessalonians 5:1-3

Also Read:

Matthew 24:36

Matthew 24:43-44

When will the Lord return?

Reread: 1 Thessalonians 5:4

Also read: Matthew 25:13

How should believers live in the face of this knowledge?

Reread: 1 Thessalonians 5:4-8

How should the promise of Christ's second coming have upon how a person lives day to day?

There is quite a contrast between believers and unbelievers.

From the five verses we just read, please list below some primary characteristics of believers as well as those of unbelievers. In some instances these will simply be in direct contrast.

Characteristics of Believers

1.

2.

3.

4.

5.

6.

7.

8.

9.

10.

11.

Characteristics of Unbelievers

1.

2.

3.

4.

5.

6.

7.

8.

9.

10.

11.

Reread: 1 Thessalonians 5:6-8

Also read:

Matthew 24:43-44

Mark 13:33-36

What should we do to get ready for the Lord's return?

Read: Luke 12:1-48

What else do we learn from these verses?

What will happen to those who are unprepared for the Lord's return?

Read the following verses as you construct your answer.

Matthew 24:37-39

Luke 17:26-27

Luke 17:28-30

Matthew 24:40

Larry Norman, "the Father of Christian Rock," wrote a song that became popular throughout the world and was sung from concerts to churches to campfires entitled *I Wish We'd All Been Ready*. He attempted to incorporate the biblical prophecies about this coming time in history in the lyrics, which you will find below. You can still find and purchase this song electronically as well as on CD or simply find it at sites all over the internet. It was included on his album *Only Visiting This Planet*, which was selected as the second-best album in <u>*CCM Magazine*</u>'s *The 100 Greatest Albums in Christian Music*. In April 2014 it was included in a group of 25 sound recordings inducted into the <u>Library of Congress</u> <u>National Recording Registry</u>. It was the first Christian rock album to be so honored.

The lyrics follow:

<u>I Wish We'd All Been Ready</u>*

Life was filled with guns and war
And everyone got trampled on the floor
I wish we'd all been ready

Children died the days grew cold
A piece of bread could buy a bag of gold
I wish we'd all been ready

There's no time to change your mind
The son has come and you've been left behind
A man and wife asleep in bed
She hears a noise and turns her head
He's gone
I wish we'd all been ready

Two men walking up a hill
One disappears and one's left standing still
I wish we'd all been ready

There's no time to change your mind
The son has come and you've been left behind

Life was filled with guns and war
And everyone got trampled on the floor

I wish we'd all been ready

Children died the days grew cold
A piece of bread could buy a bag of gold
I wish we'd all been ready

There's no time to change your mind
How could you have been so blind
The father spoke the demons dined
The son has come and you've been left behind

You've been left behind
You've been left behind
*Used by permission

Reread: 1 Thessalonians 5:6

Also read: Titus 2:12-13

What are we encouraged to avoid?

1.

2.

3.

What else should characterize our lives?

1.

2.

3.

4.

5.

6.

7.

Reread: 1 Thessalonians 5:8

Also read: Ephesians 6:14

What roles should faith, hope and love play in our lives?

Important Note: As we said earlier, the use of the word "hope" in the Greek is the opposite of our use of the word in English. In the Greek, "hope" is a confidence, sureness, and knowledge of future things. In fact, in the Greek, the word "hope" infers a certainty stronger than knowing. It is an ultimate, internal, overpowering, all-enveloping eternal surety and truth that is absolute.

How are faith, biblical hope, and love like a breast plate on a soldier protecting us from surprise attack?

How is salvation like a helmet?

Reread: 1 Thessalonians 5:9-10

For what did God choose us?

This deserves further attention.

Read: 1 Thessalonians 1:4

What two things did Paul, Silas and Timothy say they knew about the believers in Thessalonica?

1.

2.

Note: Election in the Old Testament was generally understood as a national matter. Indeed the promises of a specific area of land to Israel were made over 200 times. This does not, of course, negate God's utilization of certain men and women as His agents in the Tanakh.

In the New Testament we achieve a fuller understanding of this. (We must remember that the New and Old Testaments fit together like a hand in a glove.) It is said that the Old Testament is revealed in the new, while the new is concealed in the old. There is really no need for any division between the Old and the New. Together they form one cohesive document we know as the Bible.

We see what at first glance appears to be God's unilateral choosing of certain individuals in the following verses:

John 13:18

John 15:16

Acts 9:15

James 2:5

2 Peter 1:10

However, there is more at work in this construct.

Read: Ephesians 1:4-5

What did God do before the world was created?

What did God intend to be the result of His action?

In his book *Evangelism and the Sovereignty of God*, J. I. Packer states that the sovereignty of God and man's responsibility is an antinomy--an appearance of contradiction between conclusions which seem equally logical, reasonable or necessary (p. 18). He continues to say that while God "orders and controls all things, human actions among them . . . He holds every man responsible for the choices he makes and the courses of action he pursues" (p.22).

Read: John 6:36-40

What promise do we see for those who come to trust in Jesus?

How did Jesus summarize His Father's will?

Note: This passage contains some concepts that are sometimes, on the surface, difficult for those of us with finite minds to understand. We see:

1. God's promise to those who come to Jesus.

2. The concept that one must come to Jesus to receive life.

3. The statements about those who have come to Him and are going to come to Him. (He already knows.)

4. The statement that the Lord wants all men and women to come to Him.

This seeming conundrum can be more fully understood as one studies the Scriptures and views them as a whole. In other words:

1. God wants all people to come to Him.

2. We must choose to come to Him.

3. The "elect" will come to Him.

4. God knows who will come to Him.

We can see this borne out in the following verses:

John 17:2

John 17:6

John 17:9

John 17:11-12

John 17:24

Ephesians 1:4-5

2 Thessalonians 2:13

1 Timothy 2:3-4

Luke 19:10

2 Peter 3:9

We also see that God makes a bona fide offer to every person in the following verses:

John 3:16

John 3:36

John 5:24

Romans 10:9

Romans 10:13

We see the concept of this antinomy working in John 6:37 where we find that all that come are received and all that are given come.

Some people find it helpful to think of this in terms of a "life parade." Imagine God, who is not bound by the constraints of time, flying in a helicopter high above a parade of the events that will make up your life. He knows the beginning from the end, He knows the way He wants you to go, and yet you have a choice.

Does this concept seem difficult to understand? No wonder.

See:

- Isaiah 55:8-9

- Ephesians 3:18

Read: Ephesians 1:5

What did God decide in advance for those who come to Him by trusting in Yeshua Hamaschiah, the Jewish Messiah, who we know as Jesus?

Let's take a moment and further attempt to make two words about the future, God's foreknowledge and their meaning more clear, drawing upon insights from Warren Wiersbe.

3. The first word is "predestination." As this word is used in the Bible it refers primarily to what God does and will do for people who have come to know Him through a personal relationship with Jesus Christ. <u>Nowhere in the Judeo Christian Scriptures does it indicate that anyone is predestined to hell. The word is used only in relationship to God's people.</u> For example, God's purpose for history and believers as He has already decided relates to:

    *   The crucifixion (Acts 4:25-28).

    *   Our adoption into the family of God (Ephesians 1:5).

    *   Our conformity to Jesus (Romans 8:29-30).

    *   Our future inheritance (Ephesians 1:11).

4. The second word is "election," which refers to people, their choices and God's foreknowledge as already discussed.

We should then realize that:

3. Nobody is saved without choosing to be saved. Nobody is lost without choosing to be lost.

4. God's desire is to save as many people as possible, not as few people as possible. We see this truth all over the pages of God's Word.

Reread: 1 Thessalonians 5:9-10

For what reason can we be assured of our salvation?

How many of your sins were yet future when Jesus was crucified?

What does this mean to you?

Reread: 1 Thessalonians 5:11

How should a believer use the information in the primary passage for today to help others?

How can talking about God's fulfilled promises from the past encourage us in our daily lives?

How can talking about God's promises for the future encourage us in our daily lives?

Application Questions

What can you do to be sure you are ready for Christ's return each day??

What hope can you share with someone who is convinced that death is the end of our existence?

Close in Prayer

MORE CONCERN FOR THE THESSALONIANS
1 THESSALONIANS 5:12-28

Open in Prayer

Group Warm-Up Questions

What instructions would you give to someone taking care of your home while you were away on a long vacation?

If you could ask God any three questions about how to live your life, what would you ask?

Read: 1 Thessalonians 5:12-28

Reread: 1 Thessalonians 5:12-13

How does God want us to regard church leaders?

Please make a list from the text.

1.

2.

3.

What qualifier do we see required of church leaders to receive such honors?

Read:

Romans 12:6-8

1 Corinthians 12:1-30

As in life, God gives everyone certain gifts. Some people are qualified to act as leaders in groups of believers and some have other gifts.

Looking at Scripture we find a number of references to the qualities that make one a good leader in the family of God. Please take a look at the following references and jot down what you see. (The overlap you see is on purpose.)

Matthew 9:37-38

1 Timothy 3:6

1 Timothy 5:22

1 Samuel 13:14

1 Timothy 3:1-7

Titus 1:5-9

Titus 1:9

Colossians 1:28-29

Acts 20:28

Hebrews 13:17

1 Peter 5:2

Ezekiel 34

Galatians 1:1

Ephesians 1:1

What are we to do if confronted with church members or leaders who do not live up to the biblical standard?

Reread: 1 Timothy 1:18-19

What two primary directives did Paul give Timothy?

1.

2.

Does this also apply to us today? How so?

This verse says that some people have deliberately violated their consciences. How might they have done this?

What is the significance of the Scripture telling us that this violation of their consciences was "deliberate?"

Why is it so important that we realize this violation was an overt action of the will of these people?

What was the result when these people violated their consciences?

What do you take this to mean?

What happens when people do this today? Please think of an example and discuss:

1. What it means for the people who do this.

2. What it means for the community of believers with whom they are associated.

3. How it impacts the non-believers who are always observing the lives of believers.

Read: Philippians 4:8

This verse taken in concert with 1 Timothy 1:19 infers that clinging to one's faith in Jesus and keeping one's conscience clear is also a matter of the will. What are your thoughts about this?

Reread: 1 Timothy 1:20

What two examples does Paul give of people who violated their consciences?

What two actions did Paul take when these people made such a negative choice?

Note: In this type of instance it appears that the type of people in question have made an overt decision to go beyond the remedies available to them as referenced in:

James 5:16

Romans 12:2

Now Read:

Proverbs 13:20

Proverbs 14:7

Proverbs 25:26

Psalm 1:1-4

Psalm 119:115

Psalm 26:4-5

1 Corinthians 5:11-13

1 Corinthians 5:13

2 Corinthians 6:14

2 Peter 3:17

Numbers 16:1-35

How should we respond today when people in a group of believers also make such negative choices?

If we respond in accordance with Scripture as Paul did what impact does it have upon the faithful believers in the group?

How does it impact a group of believers if we respond in direct contradiction to the Scriptures in a disobedient and weak minded fashion, allowing these people to remain as active participants, treating them as legitimate and faithful followers?

How does it impact the effectiveness of the group if these people who have violated and continue to violate their consciences are seen by nonbelievers as representatives of what it means to be followers of Jesus?

Please discuss examples of when you have seen this handled in both ways and the impact it had.

Read:

Colossians 3:23-24

Colossians 4:5-6

Ephesians 4:29-30

What further light do these verses shed upon this subject?

How can you show respect for the legitimate and obedient elders of the group of believers of which you are a part (commonly called a "church")?

What can you do to live at peace with the other believers in the group to which you belong?

Why is this so important?

How can the peace between believers in a group be damaged?

Reread: 1 Thessalonians 5:13-15

How does God want us to treat each other?

Please make another list.

1.

2.

3.

4.

5.

6.

7.

8.

Now, go back over the items on this list one by one and discuss why:

1. Each description of one's conduct is important.

2. What impact it has on other believers and unbelievers if we act as instructed.

3. What impact it has on unbelievers and believers if we do not act as instructed.

Reread: 1 Thessalonians 5:14

What situations tend to test your patience?

Why do you think this is so?

How do you end up handling situations of this nature?

How do you plan to handle such situations when they occur in the future?

Reread: 1 Thessalonians 5:15

What happens when you pay back evil to a person who has done wrong to you?

Can you, or should you, forgive such a person?

Read: John 20:23

Note: A literal understanding of the Greek translated to English as it relates to this verse would read: "Whosoever sins you forgive shall have already been forgiven, and whosoever sins you do not forgive shall have already not been forgiven them." (KJV 1900)

Commenting on this verse and the original Greek, Warren Wiersbe said, "In other words, the disciples did not provide forgiveness; they proclaimed forgiveness on the basis of the message of the gospel."

Read the following verses to see this borne out:

Matthew 16:19

Matthew 18:18

What prerequisite do we see in John 20:23 for the apostles exercising this privilege as it relates to the Holy Spirit?

What danger lurks if people mistakenly think they have this power and authority to forgive sins on their own?

We must remember that only God can forgive sin.

See:

Mark 2:7

Acts 10:43

Acts 13:38

John 20:23

While we see that only God, through Jesus Christ, can forgive sins, who or what are believers today to forgive? Read the following verses as you construct your answer:

Luke 17:3-4

Ephesians 4:32

Colossians 3:12-13

From these verses, what must happen for the forgiveness cycle to be complete?

What if the forgiveness cycle is not complete and the one who is forgiven does not change their ways?

Why must we forgive others even if they do not change their behavior?

What impact does it have upon a human being if they harbor a spirit of unforgiveness?

Avi Lipkin, who formerly held the generals rank in the Israeli Defense Forces says, "Not forgiving others is like preparing a vial of poison for someone else and then drinking it yourself." What are your thoughts about his statement?

Even though a believer releases harmful bitterness through forgiveness, must the transgressor still bear the consequences of their action? How so?

What is the tightrope a believer must walk when in the position of delivering consequences for someone's poor behavior while at the same time forgiving them? Please explain and think of an example.

How can you forgive such a person or situation in a fashion that brings about truth and justice?

This is yet another important component in the life of a believer.

Read the following verses and note after each what God's Word says about how we ought to live, about justice and the part of those who follow Him.

Matthew 17:24-27

Matthew 22:15-22

Ephesians 2:10

Romans 12:1

Romans 8:9

James 1:22

James 2:17

James 2:26

John 15:8

Acts 1:8

Romans 12:2

Luke 6:27-28

Deuteronomy 24:17

Deuteronomy 27:19

Matthew 25:40

James 1:27

Isaiah 1:17

Isaiah 56:1

Proverbs 21:15

Hosea 12:6

Psalm 106:3

Zechariah 7:9

Proverbs 21:3

Deuteronomy 16:20

Jeremiah 22:3

Amos 5:24

Reread: 1 Peter 2:15

What kind of lives should believers live?

How does it impact the enemies of believers if they live and act as God desires?

There is an old extra-biblical proverb that says fool me once, shame on you. Fool me twice, shame on me. How might you apply this to times when you are faced with difficult situations or people?

This is an important topic as we examine our own lives and those around us. The incorrect notion or lie that those following Jesus Christ should not discern right from wrong has been responsible for the decline of the culture where it has been applied.

Unbelievers, if they know one verse, often love to quote Matthew 7:1 and take it to mean that there are no standards of behavior to which one can hold oneself or others. (For greater context see the full quote in Matthew 7:1-3.)

This is, of course, patently misunderstood and quoted out of context. As we have said before, one verse theology is essentially no theology at all. God's Word must be viewed and understood as a whole and must not be twisted by human emotions and desires.

In the Nazarene denomination this was often summarized by telling parishioners that while they were not to judge people, they were to be fruit inspectors.

So what is a believer to do?

First, we must realize that Biblical standards of conduct, speech, behavior, relationships and life are rampant in the New and Old Testaments. When these principles are applied to one's life the result is always good. Justice, truth, love, peace, joy, and fulfillment always follow although believers must take a stand for God's standards to make it happen.

Conversely, when these principles are violated, one reaps only negative consequences in the long run, despite possible periodic short term gains.

It is easy enough for a Biblically literate person to view their own life and know if they are exhibiting the fruit of the spirit as succinctly delineated in Galatians 5:22-23. If one does this they can then easily reapply the admonition found in this very letter in 1 Thessalonians 5:16-22.

Going a little bit further, read the following verses dealing with discernment and discuss what they mean to us as students of God's Word and followers of His plan and Messiah:

Romans 12:2

2 Timothy 3:16-17

Hebrews 4:12

1 Corinthians 2:14

Proverbs 8:8-9

Hosea 14:9

Romans 12:9

1 Kings 3:9-12

Proverbs 1:1-2

Proverbs 3:21-24

Ecclesiastes 12:13-14

Ephesians 4:14

Philippians 1:9-10

James 3:17

Reread: 1 Thessalonians 5:16-22

What attitudes does Paul mention as representing God's will for us? Please list them in order.

1.

2.

3.

4.

5.

6.

7.

8.

God has herein provided a "handy dandy" list that will help lead to a fruitful and successful life for a believer.

My very strong suggestion is that everyone who has trusted Jesus Christ memorize these verses and pray through them on a daily basis. This has been quite helpful to a number of people who have followed Jesus Christ for years. Why do you think this might be so?

Read: Galatians 5:22-23

How do these verses, which each of us ought to also memorize, relate to and complement 1 Thessalonians 5:16-22?

How is work of the Holy Spirit in the life of a believer enhanced by the reading and memorization of God's Word?

How should you respond to such a person or situation that has wronged you, going forward with the knowledge of what you have learned from previous experience and God's Word?

Reread: 1 Thessalonians 5:16

When should we be joyful?

How do you define the difference between joy and happiness?

Many people have said and some dictionaries confirm that joy is a deeper seated feeling of contentment emanating from within while happiness is more circumstantial. Do you agree with this?

If you could improve upon these definitions and differential how would you do it?

How can you remain joyful when things seem to be going badly?

Reread: 1 Thessalonians 5:17

When should we pray?

In practical terms, how can one do this?

How does one pray when at work, on a phone call, engaged in a conversation, at a recreational event?

How does prayer relate to a person's joy?

Reread: 1 Thessalonians 5:18

When are we to be thankful?

What is the difference between being thankful "in" all circumstances and being thankful "for" all circumstances?

While we are not told to be thankful for all circumstances, we are to be thankful in them. How can one do this?

How does it impact one's life when they are, in fact, thankful in a difficult circumstance instead of resenting it?

Read: Romans 8:28

What light does this shed on the concept of being thankful in all circumstances in the life of a believer?

What value do you then see in the life of a believer when one gives thanks as directed in the Scriptures?

Reread: 1 Thessalonians 5:19

How is it possible for someone to stifle the Holy Spirit? Please think of an example you might have seen or heard about?

Have you ever stifled the Holy Spirit?

What remedy does God provide for us if we make this mistake?

How and when can we re-appropriate the power the Holy Spirit?

Reread: 1 Thessalonians 5:20-21

Also read: Acts 17:10-11

Prophecies when understood in the context of this passage amount to the speaking forth of God's Word. If someone is expounding upon God's Word we must be sure that it is consistent with His written Word as found in the Bible.

How did the people in Berea as mentioned in Acts test even the preaching of Paul?

How should we do the same thing when listening to anyone speak?

To what should we pay attention and what should we do if we find inconsistencies in what someone is trying to tell us God's Word says?

Read 2 Timothy 3:16-17 as you think about your answer.

How can we test all things against the crucible of God's Word just like the Bereans?

How can we effectively perform such tests if we are not personally steeped in the Word of God on a daily basis?

Why, then, is it so imperative that we read, study and pray about God's Word on a daily basis? Read the following verses as you construct your answer.

Deuteronomy 6:4–9

Acts 17:11

1 Timothy 4:13

Matthew 4:4

Luke 4:4

Deuteronomy 11:18–21

Colossians 3:16

1 Timothy 4:15

John 5:39

Proverbs 23:12

Joshua 1:8

Proverbs 3:1–3

Ephesians 6:11–17

Matthew 22:29

Ephesians 6:17

Reread: 1 Thessalonians 5:22

What else are we instructed to do on an ongoing basis?

Does this extend even to the appearance of wrongdoing when we are not?

What impact does not adhering to this admonition have upon a person?

What impact does following this directive have?

Reread: 1 Thessalonians 5:23

What impact does God want to have upon us? There are a number of aspects to this referenced or alluded to in this verse. If we look hard enough we can find at least five. Please list them.

1.

2.

3.

4.

5.

For how long does God want us to enjoy these benefits?

Reread: 1 Thessalonians 5:24

Who can make these characteristics a reality for us?

How do we know this?

How can we tell if God is actually at work in us?

How can we help or hinder God's work within us?

We have already dealt to some degree with prayer and the study of God's Word as this process progresses. Read the following verses to see if there are any other components that stick out.

Hebrews 10:24-25

Ecclesiastes 4:9-12

Proverbs 27:17

Matthew 18:20

Acts 2:42

Romans 10:10

Colossians 4:5-6

Should we see characteristics spoken of in God's Word start to become realities in our lives?

Personal Note: When I became a believer many years ago I didn't know one other human being on a personal basis who I thought was also a true follower of Jesus Christ. (I should mention that I did and had been attending church and Sunday morning classes for some time.) At that point I felt pretty sure that Billy Graham was one, but that was as far as it went.

So after I made a decision, based at that point largely on John 16:33, I began to read my Bible and pray on a daily basis with a real hunger for God's Word, wisdom, and influence in my life. I found out several things. First, I found out that even though I was trying to live the way I thought was right, I was doing just about everything wrong. Second, I developed spiritually and studied the Bible. As I did so I found that when I got to certain portions and learned about the results of having the Holy Spirit in one's life I could look back and see when and where these things had already started to change in accord with the Scriptures. This was simply amazing to me and still is.

Reread: 1 Thessalonians 5:25

What request did Paul make of the believers in Thessalonica?

Why do you think Paul felt the need to make this request?

Reread: 1 Thessalonians 5:26

How would you describe the kind of affection Paul had for the believers in Thessalonica?

Reread: 1 Thessalonians 5:27

Also read: Romans 1:16

With whom did Paul instruct the Thessalonians to share his letter?

Why do you think it was so important that the contents of this letter be shared as Paul instructed?

Reread: 1 Thessalonians 5:28

Note: The Biblical definition of grace is defined as getting what you don't deserve.

Mercy is defined as not getting what you do.

What was Paul's final wish for the Thessalonian believers at the close of this letter?

Why was this so important?

Application Questions

Which of God's short, direct commands in this passage do you most need to remember this week?

With whom do you need to make peace? How can you start?

Close in Prayer

Introduction to Paul's Second Letter to the Thessalonians
The Persecutions Begin

The second letter to the believers in Thessalonica was written only a few months after the first. Some people find this proximity surprising or even confusing given the wide scope of Paul and his companion's travels and the many groups with which they were sharing their faith. Add to this their work in bolstering the faith of those who had trusted Jesus Christ and it is hard to imagine being busier.

While we don't generally realize it, the actual officially endorsed systematic lethal persecutions of those following "The Way" had begun, and these difficulties started in Thessalonica.

We see this referenced in the works of Pliny the Elder. Officially known as Gaius Plinius Secundus, Pliny was born in 23 or 24 AD and died at the relatively young age of 55 in AD 79. His accomplishments during his lifetime are somewhat staggering and if he had born later he might have been known as a "Renaissance Man."

His many endeavors included acting as an army commander, a naval commander, a naturalist, and a philosopher. He was a personal friend of the Roman emperor Vespasian and spent his spare time as an author studying, investigating, and writing about history, current events, nature and geographical phenomena.

Pliny the Elder's writings included a twenty-two volume set entitled The History of the German Wars and his Natural History which contained over one million words in thirty-seven volumes. (According to some scholars, his Natural History was essentially the first Encyclopedia.) In his quest for knowledge he attempted to document all known facts at the time and is said to have included over 20,000 pieces of information on an amazing array of topics.

So far as we know, he did not ever become a believer, although he did research faith in Jesus as a relatively honest observer. In retrospect, it would have been quite interesting for this brilliant man to have met and interacted with Paul, perhaps the most highly educated and intelligent man of the day, on a personal basis.

Speaking of those following Jesus Christ he said that they "bind themselves by oath, not to some crime, but not to commit fraud, theft, or adultery, not falsify their trust, nor to refuse to return a trust when called upon to do so." This would certainly seem to be an attempt at honestly appraising believers.

Back in Thessalonica a sort of strange practice had developed. People would offer a cask of wine on the altar of either Venus or Caesar. (Note that by this time Caesar had been deified.) Those making the offering would then take the wine back from the altar, took it to the open markets and sprinkled it over the food and other items available there announcing that his meant it had all been dedicated to the god on whose altar it had been offered. Of course, while it had been "dedicated" to the false god, the proceeds of the sales of merchandise were not in what some would deem a hypocritical and devious practice.

It was then said by the believers that a person who bought or consumed any of the items that had been sprinkled was worshipping a false god. Followers of Jesus Christ then stopped shopping at the market place and this economic impact led to the beginning of some of the first great persecutions. This included persecutions resulting in the death of believers by burning and crucifixion.

Speaking of the beginnings of these persecutions in Thessalonica, Pliny the Elder said "It was in Thessalonica that the first Gentiles were killed in the Roman Empire. The local Roman governor in that part of the country said that every Christian had to bow before a statue of Augustus Caesar. He had been deified and statues of Caesar were erected everywhere. Christians who didn't obey the edict were persecuted."

In addition, there had arisen some problems within the fellowship of believers itself when a specious and forged letter circulated among them. This letter took prophetic claims about the "Day of the Lord" out of context and was confusing some people who were operating without a good working knowledge of God's Word. Paul, Silan and Timothy were also writing to set these people on the right track, help them to access the Scriptures in their entirety, and aid them in living victorious lives as followers of the Jewish Messiah.

WEEK 8

CONCERN FOR THE THESSALONIANS
2 THESSALONIANS 1:1-12

Open in Prayer

Group Warm-Up Questions

What experiences can destroy a person's desire to live?

What fictional or real-life person endured difficulties and trials on the way to eventual triumph?

Read: 2 Thessalonians 1:1-12

Reread: 2 Thessalonians 1:1

To whom is this letter addressed?

Who wrote this letter?

Reread: 2 Thessalonians 1:2

What particular two things did the writers of this letter wish for the believers in Thessalonica?

How would you define these two things?

Read:

Ephesians 2:8-9

John 16:33

Grace is defined as getting what you don't deserve.

Mercy is defined as not getting what you do.

One of the great legal minds and students of history of the past two thousand years was John Selden who lived in England from 1584 until his death in 1654. His personal library alone held over 8,000 volumes. Upon his death bed he is reported to have said: "I have surveyed much of the learning that is among the sons of men, and my study is filled with books and manuscripts on various subjects. But at present, I cannot recollect any passage out of all my books and papers whereon I can rest my soul, save this from the sacred Scriptures:

"For the grace of God has been revealed, bringing salvation to all people."

(Titus 2:11 KJV 1900).

Why do you think grace and peace in particular were wished for the Thessalonians?

Why do you think grace is normally mentioned before peace?

Is grace a partial prerequisite for inner peace? How so?

Can you think of any examples of these principles operating in your life?

Reread: 2 Thessalonians 1:3

Also read: Romans 12:9

Why did the writers of this letter thank God for the church in Thessalonica?

The original language makes it appear that the thanks Paul, Silas and Timothy have for the Thessalonians is like the payment of a debt. They are bound to do it. What might this mean?

What can we do to keep our faith growing?

Please consider the following verses as you think about your answer:

2 Timothy 3:16-17

Hebrews 4:12

Hebrews 10:25

1 Thessalonians 5:17

Colossians 4:5-6

What can we do to increase our love for others?

Read:

1 Thessalonians 3:12

1 Thessalonians 4:1

1 Thessalonians 4:10

How do these verses from the first letter to the Thessalonians bear upon what we are reading in the second letter?

How can thanking God for the progress of other believers affirm and encourage them without puffing them up?

How can we grow in faith each day?

How can we be sure to trust God in <u>all</u> things?

How can we be sure that our lives as believers are ruled by what is important, according to God's standards, and not what is urgent?

Reread: 2 Thessalonians 1:4

Note: Remember that when this letter was written Paul and his compatriots were in Corinth experiencing their own difficult situation.

What was the reputation of the believers in Thessalonica?

What difficulties were the believers in Thessalonica experiencing?

Reread: 2 Thessalonians 1:5

Also read:

Romans 5:3-5

2 Timothy 3:12

2 Timothy 2:12

What things does persecution for one's work as an obedient believer show?

How exactly do you see this working?

How can a person go through trials and yet have their faith strengthened?

How do we know God has not forgotten us when we are going through difficulties?

What are some reasons we think of to explain why we experience trials and hard times?

How can trials and persecution possibly be part of God's permissive will and plan for us?

Reread: 2 Thessalonians 1:6-7

Also read: Romans 12:19

How will God deal with those who persecute believers?

Have you ever seen this in action? How so?

How will God deal with believers who are suffering persecution for the sake Him?

Do you think this also applies to those who stand up for God's Word and the principles found in it?

Have you seen this kind of thing in action? How so?

Do the results spoken of in these two verses always come about immediately or are they sometimes delayed?

Why do you think they might sometimes be delayed?

Read the following verses as you think about your answer.

Numbers 14:18

Exodus 34:6

Romans 2:4

2 Peter 3:9

Reread: 2 Thessalonians 1:7

When will God reward and punish people?

Reread: 2 Thessalonians 1:8

Also read: Isaiah 66:15

For what reason will God punish people?

God's response, which we see here, is not vengeance or vindictiveness but the simple administration of unwavering justice.

As we know, this is what we all deserve, but God has provided a clear way out for us.

See:

Ephesians 2:8-9

Romans 3:23

Romans 6:23

Romans 10:10

Why do and will some people refuse the lifeline and life God has and is offering them?

As an aside, we should also note that to be consistent with His character God must and will keep his unconditional covenants.

See the following verses for an expansion upon this:

1. God's Covenant with Abraham and the Jews.

- Genesis 12:3

2. God's promise of specific land.

- Genesis 12:7

- Genesis 13:15-16

- Genesis 17:7-8

3. God's promise of land, a kingdom and His Messiah.

- Psalm 89:27-37

4. God's promise of restoration to the land from a worldwide dispersion and His Messianic kingdom.

- Jeremiah 31:31-37

5. God's promise that a remnant of the Israelites will be "saved."

- Romans 11:25-29

- Zechariah 13:8-9

- Isaiah 10:20-22

Reread: 2 Thessalonians 1:9

How is the punishment of those who reject Jesus Christ described?

How is this different from popular conceptions in our culture?

Why do you think so many misconceptions about separation from God exist that seem to incorrectly minimize the experience?

According to Scripture, spending one's eternity in Hell is absolutely the worst, the most painful and the most terrifying thing that can happen to a person.

How might people respond if they realized this?

Why do believers need to pay attention to this and realize the terrible jeopardy in which their non-believing family and friends are living?

What impact does it have when one realizes the reality of the results of one's choice as they relate to Jesus Christ?

Reread: 2 Thessalonians 1:10

What will believers experience when Jesus returns?

Reread: 2 Thessalonians 1:11

How should believers be living?

What does this mean to you?

How can believers receive the power to live their lives in this fashion?

Read Galatians 5:22-23 as you think about your answer.

How do we discover God's purpose for our lives?

Reread: 2 Thessalonians 1:12

How is the name of Jesus honored in day to day life?

What happens to believers when they play their part in this?

What happens when believers do not do their part in this?

Reread:

2 Thessalonians 1:2

2 Thessalonians 1:12

How do you see these verses working or not working together?

How will our view of the trials during our life be different after Jesus returns?

Application Questions

How could your life glorify the name of Jesus this week?

In what trials and difficulties do you need patience and perseverance this week to see God's eventual good results?

What lessons do you think God is trying to teach you through the trials and difficulties you have experienced recently?

Close in Prayer

WEEK 9

THE END IS COMING
2 THESSALONIANS 2:1-12

Open in Prayer

Group Warm-Up Questions

What would make you think that the end of the world was near?

If you were convinced that the world would end in six months, what would you do until then?

What evidence do you see of evil forces active in the world today?

Read: 2 Thessalonians 2:1-12

Reread: 2 Thessalonians 2:1

What subject was Paul addressing?

Reread: 2 Thessalonians 2:2

What was upsetting some of the believers in Thessalonica?

Where did the fallacious information bothering the Thessalonians come from?

Why do such problems occur when we stray from reliance on the definitive Word of God as presented in the Judeo-Christian Scriptures, which we call the Bible?

Read:

James 3:1

Revelation 22:18-19

Just how serious a problem is it when one purposely misleads others in relation to the Word of God?

As we can see, this is actually a life and death matter of eternal proportions. The adherence to, power and veracity of the Word of God is paramount for us to realize. Read the following excerpts from Scripture that provide just a few important reminders.

2 Timothy 3:16-17

Psalm 12:6

Psalm 19:7-11

Psalm 25:4-5

Psalm 25:9-10

Psalm 33:4

Psalm 40:8

Psalm 56:4

Psalm 56:11

Palm 93:5

Psalm 94:12

Psalm 96:12-13

Psalm 111:7-8

Psalm 112:1

Psalm 119

Psalm 147:19-20

Hebrews 4:12

How would you summarize these verses and passages in your own words?

How should a believer react to any predictions about the return of Jesus?

Reread: 2 Thessalonians 2:3

Also read: Matthew 24

Why do you think the Thessalonians are cautioned again in two successive verses to not be fooled?

Why are people sometimes fooled about such things?

What must happen before the Lord returns?

How close do you think we are to the end times and the return of Jesus Christ?

What can a person do to get ready for the return of The King? (Jesus Christ, Yeshua Hamaschiach, the Jewish Messiah)

Read: Matthew 25:1-13

What do we learn from this passage about being ready?

What gives believers confidence as they face the "end times" and the growing power of what are or will be forces of the anti-Christ?

Reread: 2 Thessalonians 2:3-4

What do we learn about the personage known elsewhere in Scripture as "The Anti-Christ, The Beast, or the Man of Lawlessness?" Please make a list of what we see in these two verses alone.

1.

2.

3.

4.

5.

6.

This evil man is referenced throughout the scriptures. While we tend to refer to him as the anti-Christ, we see him called by many other names. So that we better understand what the world should expect from him let's take a brief look at a few of the Biblical references that tell us more about him.

At your convenience you may want to look up the following verses and discuss how they allude or point to this personage. You may get even more out of this exercise by including the KJV as one of the Bible translations you utilize to review these references.

Old Testament

- Genesis 3:13-15 (The Seed of the Serpent)

- Zechariah 11:16-17 (Idol Shepherd)

- Daniel 7:8-11 (Little Horn)

- Daniel 7:21-26 (Little Horn)

- Daniel 8:9-12 (Little Horn)

- Daniel 8:23-25 (Fierce King and Master of Intrigue)

- Daniel 9:26 (Prince that Shall Come, *KJV*)

- Daniel 11:36 (Willful King)

New Testament

- Revelation 11:7 (The Beast)

- 1 John 2:22 (Antichrist)

- 2 Thessalonians 2:3 (Man of Sin)

- 2 Thessalonians 2:3 (Son of Perdition)

- John 5:43 (One coming in his own name)

- 2 Thessalonians 2:8 (Man of Lawlessness)

Personal Characteristics

- An intellectual genius (Daniel 8:23, Ezekiel 28:3)

- A persuasive Speaker (Daniel 7:20, Revelation 13:2)

- A crafty politician (Daniel 11:21, Daniel 8:25)

- A financial genius (Revelation 13:16-17)

- A forceful military leader empowered by Satan (Daniel 8:24, Revelation 6:2, Revelation 13:4)

- A deceptive and ingenious religious leader (2 Thessalonians 2:4, Revelation 13:3, Revelation 13:13-14)

Physical Description

- Zechariah 11:17

Reread: 2 Thessalonians 2:5

When had the Thessalonians heard about the prophecies of the return of the Messiah?

How much had they been told?

Why do you think they were being led astray?

What needed to happen for their previous Bible study sessions to "stick?"

Why is clear Scriptural material relating to the "end times" so often ignored by the "modern" church?

What problems can arise when clear prophecies in Scripture are ignored?

Read: 2 Timothy 3:16-17

What good things result when all of Scripture is taken as a whole and utilized as presented to us in God's Word in the victorious lives of believers?

1.

2.

3.

4.

5.

6.

7.

Reread: 2 Thessalonians 2:6

What was delaying the man of lawlessness from coming to the fore on the world stage?

Reread: 2 Thessalonians 2:7

What will happen to allow the man of lawlessness to be revealed?

What powers of lawlessness and rebellion are already present in our world?

Note: This verse is generally taken to mean that the restraint mentioned is personified by believers and the power of the Holy Spirit in their lives. After the event known as the Rapture, this restraint will no longer be operating in the world. However, it will not be gone forever. A diligent study of the book of Revelation as well as the rest of God's Word reveals that the greatest revival of all time will take place after this event. During this seven year period of time known as the Tribulation, the conflict between good and evil, God and Satan, will be at the fore and there will be no doubt about what is going on. It will essentially culminate as recorded in Revelation 17:14 and beyond. Those becoming believers during those terrible days appear to have the power of the Holy Spirit available to them and this appears to empower God's people as they engage in this cosmic battle. Without the indwelling of the Holy Spirit these tribulation believers would not be able to stand against the enemy on their own power. See the following verses and consider them in light of these things:

John 14:16-17

1 Corinthians 3:16

1 Corinthians 6:19

Galatians 5:22-23

John 15:26

John 16:13-14

2 Timothy 1:7

Reread: Reread: 2 Thessalonians 2:8

What will happen when the man of lawlessness is confronted by the Lord Jesus?

How will this happen?

Reread: 2 Thessalonians 2:9-10

Whose work will the man of lawlessness be doing?

What kinds of things will this evil person be able to do? Please make a list from what you see in the text.

1.

2.

3.

4.

Note: These types of things were used by God to authenticate His message and endorse Jesus. Here we see Satan imitating them and attempting to use them to his ends. See the following verses to help understand this:

Acts 2:22

Hebrews 2:4

John 8:44

What will be the end result of these counterfeit things?

How can you decide if a miracle or miracle worker is from God or Satan?

Reread: 2 Thessalonians 2:10

Also read: John 3:19

Why will it be possible for the man of lawlessness to fool people on their way to destruction?

Why will these people willfully reject what they know to be the truth?

Why do people today so often willfully reject what they know is the truth?

Note: Sometimes today people may try to argue about the truth of God's Word. However, when confronted with facts and logic such as we can find in Composite Probability in the appendices to this book, they do not have a "leg to stand on."

Why, when confronted with incontrovertible truth and fact do those on their way to destruction then simply resort to simply saying "I don't believe that?"

Why does it even matter what these people "believe" when the truth they cannot refute contradicts what they choose to believe or the way they choose to live?

What might sometimes make people in this group of essentially belligerent unbelievers someday come to trust Jesus?

Have you ever seen an example of this? Please explain.

Reread: 2 Thessalonians 2:11-12

Also read: Proverbs 5:22

What will God do to allow those who delight in wickedness to continue in their ways?

What will cause some people to turn away from God in the *end times* when they actually need Him the most?

Read:

Ezekiel 18:23

2 Peter 3:9

1 Timothy 2:3-4

Matthew 23:37

John 3:16

John 10:10

Why does God give even those committed to wickedness the chance for a real and meaningful life?

Application Questions

How can you strengthen your faith today so that you are ready to face any evil days that will come?

Read: Ephesians 4:29

What can you say to a loved one or friend this week that will *lovingly* draw them away from wickedness and unbelief?

Close in Prayer

WEEK 10

OUR CERTAINTY
2 THESSALONIANS 2:13-17

Open in Prayer

Group Warm-Up Questions

What causes many people to give up their plans for self-improvement (diet, exercise, etc.)?

What causes some people to lose their religious faith as they grow older? (Did they have a relationship or simply a religious commitment of some type?)

If God could give you an audible word of encouragement, what would help you most?

Read: 2 Thessalonians 2:13-17

Also read:

Ephesians 1:4

2 Timothy 1:9

Romans 8:29

Romans 8:30

For what reasons did Paul and his compatriots find themselves compelled to thank God for the Thessalonian believers?

What role did God have in the Thessalonian's salvation?

When did God choose them?

What role did the Thessalonians have in choosing when, where and how to place their trust in Jesus Christ?

What role does Paul say the Holy Spirit plays in this process?

Reread: 2 Thessalonians 2:14

Acts 17:30

Proverbs 8:4

Isaiah 45:22

Isaiah 55:1

John 7:37

John 12:32

Who calls people to salvation?

Besides being called to salvation, what else are believers called to when they have this experience?

How does God work in our lives even before we put our trust in Him?

Did God use other people to help bring you to Him? Please explain.

If God used other people to help bring you to Him, have you been able to show them your gratitude? How so?

If you have not yet been able to show your gratitude to people who helped you along the way, how might you do it?

Read: Colossians 1:21-23

Note: Even during the first century AD false teachers were attempting to move people who had found new life through Jesus away from the truth of the Gospel and His Word.

What two very specific things did Paul admonish the Colossian believers to do?

Why was this so important?

Does this apply to believers today?

What particular thing did Paul warn the Colossians to not do?

Why was this so important and how does it relate to people today?

How firm is your faith?

Note: Depending on the translation of the Bible you are using we can see that the Colossians are encouraged to not move away from the "hope of the Gospel." KJV The NLT translates this as "assurance." From our first session in Colossians you might recall that the Biblical concept of hope comes from an understanding of the original language. In the Greek, "hope" is a confidence, sureness, and knowledge of future things. In fact, in the Greek, the word "hope" infers a certainty stronger than knowing. It is an ultimate, internal, overpowering, all-enveloping eternal surety and truth that is absolute.

In the case of Colossians 1:23 we must take this a step further because the verse begins with what appears to be a conditional connector. The first word in the verse is sometimes translated "If" and sometimes as "but." A cursory and out of context reading then makes it appear that if believers stand firmly in the truth of God's Word that they will be "saved" and if they do not then they will not.

This brings us to the important subject of eternal security. This is a broad and involved issue. However, a review of some of the concepts found in our study on the Gospel of John might be helpful to us as we think about this issue. To that end, let us revisit some key verses and concomitant questions.

Read: John 6:36-40

What promise do we see for those who come to trust in Jesus?

How did Jesus summarize His Father's will?

This passage contains some concepts that are sometimes, on the surface, difficult to understand. We see:

1. God's promise to those who come to Jesus.

2. The concept that one must come to Jesus to receive life.

3. The statements about those who have come to Him and are going to come to Him. (He already knows.)

4. The statement that the Lord wants all men and women to come to Him.

This seeming conundrum can be more fully understood as one studies the Scriptures and views them a whole. In other words:

1. God wants all people to come to Him.

2. We must choose to come to Him.

3. The "elect" will come to Him.

4. God knows who will come to Him.

In theology this type of occurrence is referred to as an antinomy.

In his book *Evangelism and the Sovereignty of God*, J. I. Packer states that the sovereignty of God and man's responsibility is an antinomy--an appearance of contradiction between conclusions which seem equally logical, reasonable or necessary (p. 18). He continues to say that while God "orders and controls all things, human actions among them . . . He holds every man responsible for the choices he makes and the courses of action he pursues" (p.22).

We can see this borne out in the following verses:

John 17:2

John 17:6

John 17:9

John 17:11-12

John 17:24

Ephesians 1:4

2 Thessalonians 2:13

1 Timothy 2:3-4

2 Peter 3:9

Some people find it helpful to think of this in terms of a "life parade." Imagine God, who is not bound by the constraints of time, in a helicopter flying high above a parade of the events that will make up your life. He knows the beginning from the end, He knows the way He wants you to go, and yet you have a choice.

We should also note the importance that Jesus attaches to our resurrection in the passage under consideration in this session.

See:

John 6:39

John 6:40

John 6:44

John 6:54

Why do you think Jesus continues to tell his listeners that there will be a resurrection for those who trust in Him?

What does this mean to you?

Read: John 6:41-44

Who did Jesus say would come to Him?

If we then relate this to the following passages of Scripture, it becomes even more obvious that the **endurance** spoken of in Colossians is an overt **manifestation of the reality** that one has in fact placed their trust in Jesus Christ.

Read:

1 Corinthians 15:1

1 Corinthians 15:2

Hebrews 3:6

Hebrews 10:38

Hebrews 10:39

This **endurance** is **objective** and **observable** **proof** of the reality of one's relationship with God through His Son and enjoyed in the power of the Holy Spirit.

Reread: 2 Thessalonians 2:15

2 Timothy 3:16-17

What concrete directives did Paul give the Thessalonians?

1.

2.

3.

Does this apply to us today?

How so?

How did Paul pass on these directives to the Thessalonians?

What media do we have that serves the same purpose today?

Are there any particular such resources that you find helpful? What are they?

If we access other media to aid us in our lives as believers, what simple test must it pass?

Read Acts 17:11 as you think about your answer.

One often asks what teachings a believer should be sure to hold on to as she or he lives in this world. This is an important question that has plagued people for centuries. Indeed, it had plagued the Thessalonians when they became confused about "The Day of the Lord" and whether or not He had already returned. Obviously, Scripture as a whole is the answer to this question. However, in order to assist people not yet fully conversant in the whole of God's Word, something called the *Apostles Creed* was developed many years ago. If a person goes through it line by line they can see incontrovertible basics of our faith. Each line itself is quite a summary and some of them require a bit of study to understand just what they mean. However, each line and the creed as a whole can be helpful to keep one focused on what underlining assumptions and beliefs are important to the whole. There are, in fact, some churches who repeat this creed in unison every week. While the time when this was most relevant may have passed into "high church" history, the importance of these concepts has become more vital than ever.

In some of its most popular renditions the Apostles Creed appears as below. (Please note that the reference to the "holy catholic church" in some older versions refers to all believers everywhere and not to a specific denomination.)

THE APOSTLES CREED

I believe in God the Father Almighty,

Maker of heaven and earth.

And in Jesus Christ, His only Son, our Lord;

Who was conceived by the Holy Spirit;

Born of the Virgin Mary;

Suffered under Pontius Pilate;

Was crucified, dead and buried;

He descended into Hell;

The third day He rose again from the dead;

He ascended into heaven;

And sitteth on the right hand of God the Father Almighty;

From thence He shall come to judge the living and the dead.

I believe in the Holy Spirit;

The Holy Christian Church,

the Communion of Saints;

The Forgiveness of sins;

The Resurrection of the body;

And the life everlasting.

Amen.

Note: The recitation of this creed assumes that one has made a personal commitment to Jesus Christ and wishes to have their lives made whole by the power of the Holy Spirit making them into the kind of person God intends.

Reread: 2 Thessalonians 2:16-17

Also read:

Colossians 2:7

Philippians 4:13

Galatians 5:22-23

Ephesians 4:29-30

1 Corinthians 12:13

John 16:7-11

Philippians 1:6

In what ways did Paul hope the believers in Thessalonica would be impacted?

1.

2.

3.

4.

5.

6.

7.

How does God strengthen us?

What does God do to encourage us?

What do you think weakens a person's relationship with God?

What strengthens a person's relationship with God?

What part do you think the following things play in this process?

1. Prayer:

    • See 1 Thessalonians 5:17.

2. Bible Study:

    • See 2 Timothy 3:16-17.

3. Fellowship:

    • See Hebrews 10:25.

4. The Holy Spirit:

    • See Galatians 5:22-23.

5. Telling Others:

    • See Romans 10:10.

Application Questions

What can you do this week to remind yourself every day what God has done for you?

In what area of your life would taking a firm stand for Jesus benefit you this week?

When can you make time in your schedule this week to encourage another believer? Please be specific about what you can do and when you can do it.

Close in Prayer

WEEK 11

SPECIFIC PRAYER REQUESTS
2 THESSALONIANS 3:1-5

Open in Prayer

Group Warm-Up Questions

How frequently do you stay in touch with a friend who is many miles away?

What motivates most people to pray?

Read: 2 Thessalonians 3:1-5

Reread: 2 Thessalonians 3:1

How had the gospel been received by the Thessalonians?

What aspects of how the gospel had been received by the Thessalonians did Paul hope to see elsewhere?

1.

2.

3.

Reread: 2 Thessalonians 3:1-2

What four specific things did Paul ask the Thessalonians to pray for?

1.

2.

3.

4.

How does prayer change people or circumstances?

How can prayer protect us?

How can prayer help spread the message of the gospel and God's Word?

How does our belief about God affect the way we pray?

Have you seen direct results of prayer in your life, your circumstances, or those of others? Please explain.

Reread: 2 Thessalonians 3:2

What types of people were threatening Paul?

1.

2.

Why do you think Paul differentiated and listed these characteristics differently when describing these people?

Perhaps looking at the definitions of these characteristics will be of help to us.

Evil, when attributed to a person, is often defined in terms of their behavior They are often said to:

1. Enjoy watching others in pain.

2. Have a need to control just about everything.

3. Manipulate others.

4. Hide their true intentions.

5. Show no remorse.

6. Be purposely mean to others.

7. Take no responsibility for their actions.

8. Laugh at the misfortune of others.

9. Be cruel to animals.

10. Find it funny when they insult someone.

11. Tell the truth only when it meets their needs. In other words they are purposeful and habitual liars.

Wickedness, when attributed to a person, is generally defined as going one step further and doing something known to be wrong with the *overt intent* of hurting someone else.

It is also helpful to know that Paul had and even was personally facing these same types of attacks as we see in:

Acts 17:5-9

Acts 17:13-15

Acts 18:12-17

It may give us further pause when we realize that more believers are being persecuted today around the world than at any other time in history.

For a fascinating study of this in China in the lifetime of many people engaging in this study see the book *Heavenly Man* by Brother Yun and Paul Hattaway.

Reread: 2 Thessalonians 3:3

How did Paul describe God?

What did Paul say God would do for the Thessalonians?

1.

2.

What do you think he meant when he told them what God would do for them? (He obviously wasn't promising a lack of conflict or difficulty.)

Also read:

Luke 22:31-32

Matthew 6:7-13

What will God do for people who are threatened by the evil one?

Under what conditions will He extend His protection?

Can you think of times when you have seen this in action? Please explain.

Read: Genesis 12:3

Have you seen this same principle in action in regard to Jewish people? How so?

Note: For concrete examples and understanding of this you may wish to have a member of your group present a report on *As America Has Done* by John McTiernan.

Reread: 2 Thessalonians 3:4

What confidence did Paul have in the Thessalonian believers?

How can meditating on God's love change us?

Reread: 2 Thessalonians 3:5

What technique did Paul use to remind the Thessalonians of the direction that God wants His followers to go?

Having identified this technique, what specific two things did Paul hope to see the Thessalonians do?

1.

2.

Read: Hebrews 4:15

How can thinking about Jesus' perseverance strengthen our own stance?

Application Questions

For what kind of growth in your life as a believer can you pray this week?

For whom will you pray this week that their faith will be strengthened?

Close in Prayer

WEEK 12

REQUIREMENT TO
BE PRODUCTIVE
2 THESSALONIANS 3:6-18

Open in Prayer

Group Warm-Up Questions

How does a person learn good work habits?

When have you been frustrated with a lazy person?

What kind of help do you think should be given to people who do not work?

Read: 2 Thessalonians 3:6-18

Ecclesiastes 2:24

Ecclesiastes 3:12-13

Ecclesiastes 9:10

Reread: 2 Thessalonians 3:6

Whom should we avoid?

What two main characteristics does Paul list as common to such people?

1.

2.

What kind of message does it give to non-believers when they see people who claim to be believers living useless lives?

What does it say about the faith of so called believers who waste the precious time and lives God has granted them?

What potential negative influence can associating with idle lazy people have upon the work habits of those who are attempting to be faithful?

Is this part of the reason that employers might do their best to disassociate themselves with lazy, idle, and negative employees?

1 Corinthians 6:11

1 Corinthians 15:33

What bad habits can a person develop from associating with the wrong group of friends?

Read:

Leviticus 19:12

Colossians 3:17

Is it possible that poorly led lives on the part of those who call themselves believers can bring shame upon the name of the Lord? How so?

Is it also possible that lives well lived can Glorify God? How so?

Reread: 2 Thessalonians 3:7-8

What kind of example did Paul and his companions set when visiting the Thessalonians?

What kind of an impact do you think this example made?

Reread: 2 Thessalonians 3:8

What work habits did Paul and his compatriots display that were such positive examples to the Thessalonians?

1.

2.

3.

Read: Colossians 3:24-25

What kind of motivation does God's Word tell believers should be a vital part of their time on earth?

Read:

Proverbs 22:29

Colossians 4:5-6

What kind of an impact does it have when non-believers see the excellent work of believers?

Reread: 2 Thessalonians 3:8-9

Why did Paul's group work so hard and pay for their own food?

Read 1 Corinthians 9:3-14 to see how Paul and his companions were going above in beyond in the example they were setting.

Reread: 2 Thessalonians 3:10

What rule had Paul given about working and eating?

What impact do you think it would make upon society today if that rule were to be followed in our culture?

What sort of an example should believers set for others in their lives as workers, students, parents, fellowship members, and friends?

Reread: 2 Thessalonians 3:11

What kind of reports had Paul and his companions heard about some of the so called believers in Thessalonica? What choices were these people overtly making?

1.

2.

3.

What had these people become?

Reread: 2 Thessalonians 3:12

What were the lazy and unproductive people mentioned in the previous verse commanded to do?

Reread: 2 Thessalonians 3:13

How did Paul refer to the other believers in Thessalonica who were doing their best to live in obedience to God and His Word?

What positive encouragement did he give these people?

Reread: 2 Thessalonians 3:14-15

How were the faithful Thessalonians told to regard those who refused to follow God's standard for living productive and obedient lives?

What specific actions were the faithful believers told to take in relationship to those who were not?

1.

2.

Why was this important?

What should we do with people who purposely do not follow such biblical instructions and still attempt to be regarded as full and faithful members?

What happens when discipline in the body of believers is not attended to? Please give an example, perhaps from personal observation.

What is the positive result when discipline among believers is properly addressed? Please give an example of a time when you have seen this working with success.

For more information on this important topic read:

Matthew 18:15-17

Jude 1:3-23

1 Corinthians 5:12-13

Reread: 2 Thessalonians 3:16

What final blessing did Paul invoke upon the Thessalonian believers?

Why do you think he wished this particular blessing upon them knowing what they were going through? Why was it important in their particular situation?

Reread: 2 Thessalonians 3:17

How did Paul authenticate his letter in a special way?

Reread: 2 Thessalonians 3:18

With what final thought did Paul leave his readers and what was his wish for them?

What does this mean to you?

Application Questions

What improvements in your work habits can you make this week?

What can you do this week to be a good influence on your fellow workers, associates, or students?

From what bad influences to you need to distance yourself? How?

Close in Prayer

APPENDIX 1

HOW TO AVOID ERROR

(Partially excerpted from *The Road to Holocaust* by Hal Lindsey)

1. The most important single principle in determining the true meaning of any doctrine of our faith is that we start with the clear statements of the Scriptures that specifically apply to it, and use those to interpret the parables, allegories and obscure passages. This allows Scripture to interpret Scripture. The Dominionists (and others seeking to bend Scripture to suit their purposes) frequently reverse this order, seeking to interpret the clear passages using obscure passages, parables and allegories.

2. The second most important principle is to consistently interpret by the literal, grammatical, historical method. This means the following:

    1. Each word should be interpreted in light of its normal, ordinary usage that was accepted in the times in which it was written.

2. Each sentence should be interpreted according to the rules of grammar and syntax normally accepted when the document was written.

3. Each passage should also be interpreted in light of its historical and cultural environment.

Most false doctrines and heresy of Church history can be traced to a failure to adhere to these principles. Church history is filled with examples of disasters and wrecked lives wrought by men failing to base their doctrine, faith, and practice upon these two principles.

The Reformation, more than anything else, was caused by an embracing of the literal, grammatical, and historical method of interpretation, and a discarding of the allegorical method. The allegorical system had veiled the Church's understanding of many vital truths for nearly a thousand years.

Note 1: It is important to note that this is how Jesus interpreted Scripture. He interpreted literally, grammatically, and recognized double reference in prophecy.

Note 2: It is likewise important that we view Scripture as a whole. Everything we read in God's Word is part of a cohesive, consistent, integrated message system. Every part of Scripture fits in perfectly with the whole of Scripture if we read, understand, and study it properly.

Note 3: Remember to <u>**Appropriate the power of The Holy Spirit**</u>.

Read: Luke 11:11-13   Read: I Timothy 4:15-16

Read: Luke 24:49   Read: II Peter 2:1

Read: John 7:38-39   Read: Mark 13:22

Read: John 14:14-17, 26

APPENDIX 2

UNDERSTANDING COMPOSITE PROBABILITY AND APPLYING IT TO THE JUDEO-CHRISTIAN SCRIPTURES

Before proceeding we might briefly reflect upon the reliability of the Judeo-Christian Scriptures. All honest researchers into their veracity have found that, as historical documents, they are without parallel. They are the most reliable and incontrovertibly accurate documents available in the world today. This has been the conclusion of all the erudite scholars and investigators who have taken the time to delve into this topic. For more information on this subject you may wish to read *The Case For Christ* by Lee Stroebel, *More Than a Carpenter* by Josh McDowell, and the *Evidence That Demands a Verdict* series, also by Josh McDowell. This is, of course, a very short list of the volumes available. A great deal of augmentative and corroborative material is available in such volume that if one were so inclined they might spend a lifetime in its study.

To better understand one of the ways the Creator of the Universe has validated His Word and the work and person of Jesus Christ, it is helpful to get a grasp on composite probability theory and its application to the Judeo-Christian Scriptures.

We are indebted to Peter W. Stoner, past chairman of the Department of Mathematics and Astronomy at Pasadena City College as well as to Dr. Robert C. Newman with his Ph.D. in astrophysics from Cornell University for the initial statistical work on this topic. Their joint efforts on composite probability theory were first published in the book *Science Speaks*.

Composite Probability Theory

If something has a 1 in 10 chance of occurring, that is easy for us to understand. It means that 10 percent of the time, the event will happen. However, when we calculate the probability of several different events occurring at the same time, the odds of that happening increase exponentially. This is the basic premise behind composite probability theory.

If two events have a 1 in 10 chance of happening, the chance that both of these events will occur is 1 in 10 x 10, or 1 in 100. To show this numerically this probability would be 1 in 10^2, with the superscript indicating how many tens are being multiplied. If we have 10^3, it means that we have a number of 1000. Thus 10^4 is equivalent to 10,000 and so on. This is referred to as 10 to the first power, 10 to the second power, 10 to the third power, and so on.

For example, let's assume that there are ten people in a room. If one of the ten is left handed and one of the ten has red hair, the probability that any one person in the room will be left handed and have red hair is one in one hundred.

We can apply this model to the prophecy revealed in the Bible to figure out the mathematical chances of Jesus' birth, life and death, in addition to many other events occurring in the New Testament by chance. To demonstrate this, we will consider eight prophecies about Jesus and assign a probability of them occurring individually by chance. To eliminate any disagreement, we will be much more limiting than is necessary. Furthermore, we will use the prophecies that are arguably the most unlikely to be fulfilled by chance. I think you will agree that in doing so, we are severely handicapping ourselves.

1. The first prophecy from Micah 5:2 says, "But you, O Bethlehem Ephrathah, are only a small village in Judah. Yet a ruler of Israel will come from you, one whose origins are from the distant past" (NLT). This prophecy tells us that the Messiah will be born in Bethlehem. What is the chance of that actually occurring? As we consider this, we also have to ask: What is the probability that anyone in the history of the world might be born in this obscure town? When we take into account all of the people who ever lived, this might conservatively be 1 in 200,000.

Amazingly, about 700 years after this prophecy was uttered it was fulfilled when Yeshua Ha-Maschiach (The Jewish Messiah), who we call Jesus, was born in exactly the place predicted. We see this in Luke 2:11 where it states "The Savior— yes, the Messiah, the Lord—has been born today in Bethlehem, the city of David" (NLT)!

2. Let's move on to the second prophecy in Zechariah 9:9: "Rejoice greatly, O people of Zion! Shout in triumph, O people of Jerusalem! Look, your King is coming to you. He is righteous and victorious, yet He is humble, riding on a donkey---even on a donkey's colt" (NLT). For our purposes, we can assume the chance that the Messiah (the King) riding into Jerusalem on a donkey might be 1 in 100. But, really, how many kings in the history of the world have actually done this?

The fulfillment of this particular prophecy 500 years later was so unnerving that Matthew, Mark, Luke and John all included it in their historical accounts.

Matthew recorded it as "Tell the people of Jerusalem, 'Look, your King is coming to you. He is humble, riding on a donkey— riding on a donkey's colt' " (Matthew 21:5 NLT).

This appears in John's writings as "The next day, the news that Jesus was on the way to Jerusalem swept through the city. A large crowd of Passover visitors took palm branches and went down the road to meet him. They shouted, "Praise God! Blessings on the one who comes in the name of the LORD! Hail to the King of Israel!" Jesus found a young donkey and rode on it, fulfilling the prophecy that said: "Don't be afraid, people of Jerusalem. Look, your King is coming, riding on a donkey's colt" (John 12:12–15 NLT).

3. The third prophecy is from Zechariah 11:12: "I said to them, 'If you like, give me my wages, whatever I am worth; but only if you want to.' So they counted out for my wages thirty pieces of silver" (NLT). What is the chance that someone would be betrayed and the price of that betrayal would be thirty pieces of silver? For our purposes, let's assume the chance that anyone in the history of the world would be betrayed for thirty pieces of silver might be 1 in 1,000.

As unlikely as it may have seemed on the surface, this prediction was fulfilled approximately 500 years later and was noted by Matthew with the language itself being eerily similar to what had been written so many years ago. The NLT shows this as "How much will you pay me to betray Jesus to you? And they gave him thirty pieces of silver." (Matthew 26:15) How shocking would it be if you found that someone predicted exactly what you were going to spend for your next dinner out 500 years ago?

4. The fourth prophecy comes from Zechariah 11:13: "And the Lord said to me, 'Throw it to the potter'---this magnificent sum at which they valued me! So I took the thirty coins and threw them to the potter in the Temple of the Lord" (NLT). Now we need to consider what the chances would be that a temple and a potter would be involved in someone's betrayal. For our statistical model, let's assume this is 1 in 100,000.

This prophecy and its fulfillment is a continuation and completion of the one immediately prior to it in which the exact amount of the bribe for the betrayal of the Jewish King was predicted, again 500 years before it occurred. Here we find predicted not only the betrayal and the exact payment, but the actual usage of the funds. Matthew records fulfillment of this whole process as "I have sinned," he declared, "for I have betrayed an innocent man." "What do we care?" they retorted. "That's your problem." Then Judas threw the silver coins down in the Temple and went out and hanged himself. The leading priests picked up the coins. "It wouldn't be right to put this money in the Temple treasury," they said, "since it was payment for murder." After some discussion they finally decided to buy the potter's field, and they made it into a cemetery for foreigners (Matthew 27:4-7 NLT).

5. The fifth prophecy in Zechariah 13:6 reads: "And one shall say unto him, What are these wounds in thine hands? Then he shall answer, Those with which I was wounded in the house of my friends" (KJV). The question here is, "How many people in the history of the world have died with wounds in their hands?" I believe we can safely assume the chance of any person dying with wounds in his or her hands is somewhat greater than 1 in 1,000.

Again, 500 years later we see this specific prophecy fulfilled and the evidence viewed by Jesus's disciples in John 20:20 where it says "As he spoke, he showed them the wounds in his hands and his side. They were filled with joy when they saw the Lord" (NLT)!

6. The sixth prophecy in Isaiah 53:7 states, "He was oppressed and treated harshly, yet he never said a word. He was led like a lamb to the slaughter. And as a sheep is silent before the shearers, he did not open his mouth" (NLT). This raises a particularly tough question. How many people in the history of the world can we imagine being put on trial, knowing they were innocent, without making one statement in their defense? For our statistical model, let's say this is 1 in 1,000, although it is pretty hard to imagine.

In this case, approximately 700 years passed between the time the prediction was made and we see it fulfilled in Mark 15:3-5. There it is recorded as "Then the leading priests kept accusing him of many crimes, and Pilate asked him, "Aren't you going to answer them? What about all these charges they are bringing against you?" But Jesus said nothing, much to Pilate's surprise" (NLT).

7. Moving on to the seventh prophecy, Isaiah 53:9 says "He had done no wrong and had never deceived anyone. But he was buried like a criminal; he was put in a rich man's grave" (NLT). Here we need to consider how many people, out of all the good individuals in the world who have died, have died a criminal's death and been buried in a rich person's grave. These people died out of place. (Some might also infer that they were buried out of place, though that is not necessarily true.) Let's assume the chance of a good person dying as a criminal and being buried with the rich is about 1 in 1,000.

Again we find that 700 years passed between the prediction of this event and the actual occurrence. Again, this event was so momentous that it was recorded by Matthew, Mark, Luke and John. Astonishingly, we find that he was placed in the tomb by not just one person of wealth, but by two. Joseph of Arimathea and Nicodemus, two of the wealthiest men in the region, worked together and laid the body in Joseph's own tomb. Matthew 27:60, speaking of Joseph of Arimathea's part in entombing Jesus' body says "He placed it in his own new tomb, which had been carved out of the rock. Then he rolled a great stone across the entrance and left" (NLT).

8. The eighth and final prophecy is from Psalm 22:16: "My enemies surround me like a pack of dogs; an evil gang closes in on me. They have pierced my hands and feet" (NLT). Remember this passage and all the other prophetic references to the crucifixion were written before this form of execution was invented. However, for our purposes, we just need to consider the probability of someone in the history of the world being executed by crucifixion. Certainly, Jesus wasn't the only person killed by being crucified. We will say that the chances of a person dying from this specific form of execution to be at 1 in 10,000.

Here we might note that Psalm 22 was penned by King David approximately 1000 years prior to the birth of Jesus. The word "crucifixion" and its derivatives had not yet been coined, but we see the process described in detail. Again, because of the import of this event it is recorded by each of the Gospel writers. In Mark 16:6 we see the fulfillment of the ancient prophecy and more where we read "Don't be alarmed. You are looking for Jesus of Nazareth, who was crucified. He isn't here! He is risen from the dead! Look, this is where they laid his body" (NLT).

Calculating the Results

To determine the chance that all these things would happen to the same person by chance, we simply need to multiply the fraction of each of the eight probabilities. When we do, we get a chance of 1 in 10^{28}. In other words, the probability is 1 in 10,000,000,000,000,000,000,000,000,000.

Would you bet against these odds?

Unfortunately, there is another blow coming for those who do not believe the Bible is true or Jesus is who He said He was. There are not just eight prophecies of this nature in the Bible that were fulfilled in Jesus Christ------there are *more than three hundred* such prophecies in the Old Testament. The prophecies we looked at were just the ones that we could *most easily* show fulfilled.

If we deal with only forty-eight prophecies about Jesus, based on the above numbers, the chance that Jesus is not who He said He was or the Bible is not true is 1 in 10^{168}. This is a larger number than most of us can grasp (though you may want to try to write it sometime). To give you some perspective on just how big this number is, consider these statistics from the book *Science Speaks* by Peter Stoner:

- If the state of Texas were buried in silver dollars two feet deep, it would be covered by 10^{17} silver dollars.

- In the history of the world, only 10^{11} people have supposedly ever lived. (I don't know who counted this.)

- There are 10^{17} seconds in 1 billion years.

- Scientists tell us that there are 10^{66} atoms in the universe and 10^{80} particles in the universe.

- Looking at just forty-eight prophecies out of more than three hundred, there is only a 1 in 10^{168} chance of Jesus not being who He said He was or of the Bible being wrong.

In probability theory, the threshold for an occurrence being absurd---translate that as "impossible"---is only 10^{50}. No thinking person who understands these probabilities can deny the reality of our faith or the Bible based on intellect. Every person who has set out to disprove the Judeo-Christian Scriptures on an empirical basis has ended up proving the Bible's authenticity and has, in most cases, become a believer.

These facts are more certain than any others in the world. However, not everyone who has come to realize the reliability and reality of these documents has become a believer. These intelligent people who understand the statistical impossibility that Jesus was not who He claimed to be and who yet do not make a decision for Christ are not senseless; they generally just have other issues. They allow these issues to stop them from enjoying the many experiential benefits that God offers them through His Word and the dynamic relationship they could have with Him, not to mention longer-term benefits. These people, of course, deserve love and prayer, because this is not just a matter of the intellect. If it were, every intelligent inquirer would be a believer. Rather, it is very much a matter of the heart, the emotions, and the spirit.

The truth of this statement was brought home to me in one very poignant situation. In this case, someone very near and dear to me said, "But Dad, this could have been anybody." No, this could not have been just anybody. The chance these prophecies could have been fulfilled in one person is so remote as to be absurd. That is impossible. Only one person in human history fulfilled these prophecies and that person is Jesus Christ. To claim otherwise is not intelligent, it is not smart, it is not well-considered, and it is not honest. It may be emotionally satisfying, but in all other respects it is self-delusional.

Printed in the United States
by Baker & Taylor Publisher Services